When God Calls You To Recovery

USING THE LORD'S STRENGTH TO
BREAK AND DESTROY ADDICTION

Lanier T. Northrup

TRILOGY CHRISTIAN PUBLISHERS
TUSTIN, CA

Trilogy Christian Publishers
A Wholly Owned Subsidiary of Trinity Broadcasting Network
2442 Michelle Drive
Tustin, CA 92780

Copyright © 2019 by Lanier T. Northrup

All Scripture quotations, unless otherwise noted, taken from THE HOLY BIBLE, NEW INTERNATIONAL VERSION®, NIV® Copyright © 1973, 1978, 1984, 2011 by Biblica, Inc.® Used by permission. All rights reserved worldwide.

Scripture quotations marked (KJV) taken from The Holy Bible, King James Version. Cambridge Edition: 1769.

All rights reserved, including the right to reproduce this book or portions thereof in any form whatsoever.

For information, address Trilogy Christian Publishing
Rights Department, 2442 Michelle Drive, Tustin, Ca 92780.

Trilogy Christian Publishing/ TBN and colophon are trademarks of Trinity Broadcasting Network.

For information about special discounts for bulk purchases, please contact Trilogy Christian Publishing.

Manufactured in the United States of America

Trilogy Disclaimer: The views and content expressed in this book are those of the author and may not necessarily reflect the views and doctrine of Trilogy Christian Publishing or the Trinity Broadcasting Network.

Cover image: Photo by Andrew Neel from Pexels

10 9 8 7 6 5 4 3 2 1

Library of Congress Cataloging-in-Publication Data is available.

ISBN 978-1-64088-615-5

ISBN 978-1-64088-616-2 (ebook)

Contents

Dedication v
You Never Meant for THIS to Happen 1
The Bottom 17
Stay at the Bottom or Start Climbing: It's Your Choice 47
The First Steps 65
Confronting the Skeletons in the Closet 83
Removing the Skeletons from the Closet 93
Tending to the Garden of Faith and Hope 99
Sharing an Experience with the Apostle Paul 113
God Will Handle the Details…If You Let Him 123
Hiding Behind Jesus 135
The Gift of Redemption 159
The Most Difficult Mountain to Climb: Forgiveness 183
What is Recovery? 193
Absolute Necessity of Trusting God Through Recovery 199
Forgiveness; It's Not Something to "Find" in Your Heart 211
Empty the Trash 225

Trust and Obey God's Plan for You 231

Notes 237

The Twelve Steps of Alcoholics Anonymous 239

Dedication

To the most amazing wife, children, entire family, and truest and sincerest of friends: when you had every right to walk away, you all stood beside me, lifted me back up and never quit on me. Instead of shame, humiliation and guilt, you provided love, structure and hope! "May the Lord bless you and keep you. May the Lord make His face to shine upon you and be gracious unto you and give you His peace." May you one day experience the same wondrous blessings you were to me; the blessings that saved my life.

You Never Meant for THIS to Happen

If you have picked up this book, I would venture to assume that what "called" you to this book is the fact that you or someone you love is currently standing in the most overwhelming state of confusion, stress and instability of your entire life. On top of it, you cannot even say for sure when it all started and how in the world it ever got to this point. Never once were there intentions to become hijacked and completely ruled by a drink, a pill, or any other chemical substance. In fact, you have probably always been one of those people who has condemned the addict and strongly shared your opinion that an addiction was a choice, and not a disease. You, like millions of others, have had very little sympathy for the fallen foe of dependency and believed it was nothing more than an excuse for their mental weakness. Now, you are humbly eating your words and fighting the hardest and most painful battle you have ever faced. You have spent countless hours on your knees asking your God for deliverance from the demon, and have been determined you will kill this thing on your own terms. At times, you might go days, and sometimes weeks without the pills, drink, needle, or pipe, but just when you think you might be winning and gaining an edge on it, another opportunity or temptation nips you on the heel. Some instances, you listen to the voice inside you that persuades you to swallow your pride and seek the professional help you need in order to climb out of this personal pit of hell. Nonetheless, just as quickly as you resolve to admit your ailment, you talk yourself back out of it. You reason that in no way could you divulge this complete embarrassing failure to the public, your family, and your friends. You are convinced that by revealing this unforgivable flaw, it is sure to destroy your reputation and everything for which you have worked so hard. It also would make you look weak and helpless. Maybe, you have reasoned that you don't think you could ever survive the detox and withdrawal symptoms and the thought of facing a day of reality scares the life out of you. Perhaps, you feel that recovery from your addiction is much too steep of a mountain to climb. Hence, you have held it close to your vest until the inevitable spotlight has shown it all to everyone. Your whole life's vision has now been flipped upside down. What you once had envisioned for your lifetime on this earth now seems an impossibility, and you are so unsure of what you can salvage of your future that you wonder if it is even worth living to find out.

There can't possibly be a future that includes success and happiness now that I have passed this point of no return. I have dug a hole in which I will spend the rest of my life suffering and paying for what I have done to myself.

Does this sound like a familiar conclusion at which you have arrived, or at least one that keeps haunting your thoughts as soon as you begin planning your escape from this torturous hell on earth? If so, you are completely normal and, as a matter of fact, it's a good indication that you are indeed destined for greatness. You see, the enemy only whispers in the ears, torments the soul, and tries to discourage the heart of those whom he knows have the gift from the almighty God and play a role in the Lord's grand plan. In God's plan, there are no mistakes. He takes our successes, our blunders, our worst faults, and our greatest accomplishments, and he begins to blend, mold and shape into a perfect work of art for His purpose and glory. Nothing you have done is too terrible for God to use. In fact, if you were truly beyond the point of no return and completely useless to The Father, the enemy would not waste one second whispering doubts in your ear, as his work would be complete and he would move on to the next poor soul. In all reality, the enemy is scared to death of your potential to completely destroy his vicious plans for so many like you. His whispers of doubt, guilt, doom and despair are his full-force attack to do whatever he can to stop you from pulling away from his grip and fulfilling God's wonderful planned destiny for you.

So, it is assumed that since you did pick up this book you are approaching or have arrived at what many call "the bottom." It is where Jerry stood in the book, *When God Calls You to the Principal's Office* when his only imaginable way out was a head-on collision with a semi-truck to take his life and remove him from the seemingly hopeless world he had created for himself, his family and his friends. As he describes, Jerry was standing at the doorstep of hell and all he had to do was knock.

Jerry was an educator with fifteen years under his belt and success coming at him from all directions. He was one of the hardest workers and most dedicated employees who could be found. His integrity and trustworthiness were of unmatched levels, and his honesty was as dependable as the rising of the sun. He had been promoted to the principal's chair, had been honored with one of the highest awards given to a school, and was well on his way to the superintendent's throne. His wife was a dedicated and loyal woman who put her career on hold many times to support Jerry's career ambitions. Maggie had also given Jerry two wonderful children who were excelling in the school, on the athletic fields and in the community. From the outside looking in, their life was a fairy tale model many couples envied and wished they could only have a marriage and home with just half of the happiness and blessings.

However, Jerry was human just like the rest of us and was very good at concealing his skeletons. At the young age of sixteen, Jerry was enjoying one of those rambunctious engagements that he was so well known for during his younger years. While with a couple of his friends on a one-day mountain climbing expedition outside of his hometown, he took a treacherous fall that broke a couple of bones and kicked off the undetected slow deterioration of his spine. Jerry was a tough kid who, within a few months, forced his way back onto the high school football and baseball fields, and put the incident behind him. After two decades had passed, it seemed the accident was ancient history and seldom entered Jerry's thoughts, until the old injury decided to rear its ugly head again. At the very same time he was enjoying his promotion to the head chair of the school, Jerry was also undergoing multiple spinal reconstruction and fusion surgeries. Each medical procedure rehabilitated the strength he once had and helped shed some of the pain he had been enduring. However, what he was not aware of was just how viciously the medications could hijack his life. By the end of his fourth surgery in three years, Jerry was physically back on his feet, but psychologically dependent upon the pain medications.

Now, the words "psychologically dependent" is a nice way to say, Jerry was flat out addicted to these pills. So much so that in order to get these pills, he often found himself doing things that were so far outside of his character that it made him physically ill to even think about some of them.

Within no time at all, Jerry's life became no more than a repetition of countless days that never differed from the previous one and were a simple blur of weeks, months and years. Every night he would lay his head on the pillow with regret eating at his core. Thoughts of the actions he had taken in order to obtain the day's dosage would cause him to toss and turn with guilt and disbelief. By midnight, Jerry would be convinced that this day had been the final day of this alien lifestyle, and tomorrow would be the first day of the rest of his clean life. He would promise himself to fight the temptations and be strong enough to just say "NO" to the urge. He knew it would only take a few tough days to get past the withdrawals, and then he would be home free. Convinced that he would beat this demon and tomorrow was going to be different, Jerry would finally drift off to sleep in the early morning hours and wake to his alarm clock.

While reaching for the snooze button, the first subconscious thought in his head would be a question of where he might find his daily dose. Gritting his teeth and remembering the plans from just a few short hours prior, Jerry would shake off the thought and roll back onto his pillow. Within just a few short minutes, his mind would begin racing and questioning whether he could make it through the day without the medication. He would start talking himself into "just one more." As he fought to change his focus off the pills, the torturous anxiety would begin to consume his complete being, and before the ten-minute snooze alarm would sound, he would be sitting up at the bedside, completely obsessed with conjuring up his next manipulative plan to con a daily pocketful from a kind-hearted and unsuspecting friend.

Besides secretly seeing different doctors for the same ailment, he had also become very good at showing his immense pain to others who had big hearts. Like clockwork, within just a few minutes of them inquiring about his agony and Jerry stating that he would "just have to live with it", the well-meaning coworkers or friends would bring him an entire bottle of leftover pain meds from some previous medical procedure. Counting on humans to be creatures of habit, he also quickly learned where most people stocked their medicines in their houses. Upon friendly visits to their homes, it wasn't long before Jerry would excuse himself to their bathrooms. Most of the time, the bottle of pills were exactly where he would imagine. Without any hesitation, he would slip a few in his pockets to get him by until his doctors would refill the next prescription.

As all malevolent habits do, Jerry's luck inevitably ran out. This finally came to a screeching end when Jerry's little secret was revealed and his whole world came to a crashing halt. Jerry started his morning in the same manner he always did. However, by noon on that infamous day, Jerry was without a job, facing felony-level charges, had a community of 5,000 people shocked and disappointed, and worst of all, a wife and two children who had every right and justification to cut ties and let him sink. By mid-afternoon, all hope was gone. He had devised the perfect suicide plan and was walking out the front door of his house to finish the job.

Fast forward a few years, and we see Jerry had returned to the education world, and surprisingly, returned to the same community where he successfully took the principal's chair once again and helped lead the school out of poor performance standings. He regained the love and respect of teachers, students, parents and community members and has now moved on to managing adult education and professional development efforts within a worldwide engineering and construction firm. Most importantly, he has done all this with his wife Maggie and two children, Elaine and Allen, by his side, providing the power in his sails the entire time.

So what happened in the gap of time that took Jerry from the doorstep of hell to a life that was once again full of blessings, success and overflowing family love? That is exactly what we will discuss in the following pages. However, let this be a warning right up front. There will be no sensitivity to religious beliefs or respect of political correctness. When it is a matter of life or death, we want answers and we want them straight and true, and that is exactly how you will get it.

First of all, we have to get one thing straight and understand the most important and undeniable fact: God is exactly who He says He is. He is the Alpha; the Omega. He is the one and only God, and there are no others. God is the great I AM. God has created us in His image, and not the other way around. Unfortunately, we have a terrible habit of creating a god in our minds that fits our lifestyle and our choices. We invent a god that has flawed human characteristics and who changes with the times, trends and our ever-evolving personal desires and distortions. We say that we choose to believe in a god that will accept us for who we choose to be. Sorry to burst your bubble, however your beliefs, or choice not to believe, does not change what is truth and what is real. You can *believe* all you want that there is no sun, but tomorrow morning it is going to rise in the east and later, will set in the west. Just bluntly putting it, the voice in your head telling you that God really doesn't mean what he says in the Bible, is once again the voice of the enemy. It is his deceptive attempts to lead you astray from The One True God and justifying your choice to live a life on the broad road to destruction and right into the enemy's pit. It is the same voice still playing the same old tricks as he did thousands of years ago in the Garden of Eden.

> *He said to the woman, "Did God really say that you shouldn't eat from any tree in the garden?"*
> *The woman said to the snake, "We may eat the fruit of the garden's trees but not the fruit of the tree in the*

middle of the garden. God said, 'Don't eat from it, and don't touch it, or you will die.'"

The snake said to the woman, "You won't die! God knows that on the day you eat from it, you will see clearly and you will be like God, knowing good and evil." The woman saw that the tree was beautiful with delicious food and that the tree would provide wisdom, so she took some of its fruit and ate it, and also gave some to her husband, who was with her, and he ate it.

Genesis 3: 1-6 (CEB)

The question is: are you also eating up the words from the enemy?

Jesus Christ is the same yesterday, today, and forever! Don't be misled by the many strange teachings out there. It's a good thing for the heart to be strengthened by grace rather than by food. Food doesn't help those who live in this context.

Hebrews 13: 8-9 (CEB)

The fact is that God is never changing. He is who He has always been and will always be. His expectations of His children have never changed and will never change. The narrow pathway that He has set for us to follow to heaven is not going to adapt to our lifestyles or our political biases and tolerances. Many actually believe that the creator of the universe, who is infinite in being, will simply decide to change His purest of expectations of what He deems is right, holy and true because of "changing times." This is a thousand times more absurd than believing a judge will ignore the speed limit law simply because your vehicle was engineered to reach speeds of 200 miles per hour and your belief that the traffic laws need to change and adapt according to today's vehicle capabilities. When standing in front of the judge, your argument will not earn you any sympathy or a reduction in your jail time. Likewise, when standing in front of our Heavenly Father on judgement day, our excuses and demands for God to relax his verdict because we made the critical mistake to choose to believe in a god that we created in our imaginations will do us no good. Just because our simple human minds cannot understand or grasp the ultimate plan of our omnipotent Creator, it does not miraculously free us to choose not to believe the truth and to deny God, but yet to attempt to "shame" or "guilt" The LORD into giving us a free pass into heaven because we did not agree with His means. Sorry, it just does not work that way.

Once you have understood this simple truth of who the Father is and of His available mercy and grace, you can move on to conquering this demon of addiction. It is understood that our 12-Step program says that "a

Power greater than ourselves could restore us to sanity," but if you are praying to any greater power other than the one true God, you might as well walk outside, search for a unique rock that feels comfortable in your hand and start praying to that pebble. Because that rock has the same power to accomplish anything that a non-existent god can do, and that is absolutely nothing. So let's get started.

Twenty Questions (Pills Anonymous)

1. Has your doctor, spouse or anyone else expressed concern about your use of medication?
2. Have you ever decided to stop taking pills only to find yourself taking them again contrary to your earlier decision?
3. Have you ever felt remorse or concern about taking pills?
4. Has your efficiency or ambition decreased since taking pills?
5. Have you established a supply for purse, pocket, or to hide away in case of emergency?
6. Have you ever been treated by a physician or hospital for excessive use of pills (whether or not in combination with other substances)?

7. Have you ever changed doctors or pharmacies for the purpose of maintaining your supply?
8. Have you received the same medication from two or more physicians or pharmacists at approximately the same time?
9. Have you ever been turned down for a refill?
10. Have you ever taken other people's pills with or without their permission or obtained them illegally?
11. Have you taken the same pain or sleep medication for a prolonged period of time only to find you still have the same symptoms?
12. Have you ever informed your physician as to which pill works best at which dosage and had them adjust the prescription to your recommendation?
13. Have you increased the dosage, strength or frequency of your pills over the past month or year?
14. Are your pills quite important to you; e.g., do you worry about refills long before running out?
15. Do you become annoyed or uncomfortable when others talk to you about your use of pills?
16. Have you or anyone else noticed a change of personality when you take your pills, or when you stop taking them?
17. Have you ever taken your medication before you had the associated symptoms?

18. Have you ever been embarrassed by your behavior when under the influence of your pills?
19. Do you ever sneak or hide your pills?
20. Do you find it impossible to stop or to go for a prolonged period without your pills?

If you answered "Yes" to three or more of these questions, then our experience would indicate that you may be one of us.

LANIER T. NORTHRUP

The Bottom

Jerry was able to meet the criteria of answering "yes" to three or more of those questions. As a matter of fact, he could answer "yes" to more than ten of the questions. In total, Jerry answered "yes" to nineteen of the twenty questions, leaving out only number six, but that would have come soon enough if it had not been for a divine intervention.

From books, counselors, pastors and interventionists, we hear one thing in common: in order for an addict to reach out for or accept help, he or she has to "hit rock bottom." Unfortunately for many, the bottom is too far because that basement floor is none other than their death. Therefore, if you are a family member or a loved one of an addict, you might want to "manufacture" the bottom as soon as possible before it is, indeed, six feet under the ground. That means you need to immediately stop enabling the addict and get ready to take everything away from him or her, including their freedom, if they are not willing to get help. In other words, it's time for an intervention. However, the manner in which the intervention is handled and portrayed will determine more than whether or not the addict will accept help. It can, and will most likely, determine the life or death of the addict!

If the intervention stands a chance of success, two things must be avoided. First, it is understood that many family members and friends have suffered some absolute heartbreaks, and saying their lives have been turned upside down is an absolute understatement! However, the focus of the conversation cannot be centered on "me". When the addict is bombarded with everything they have done to you, the interpretation of the intervention becomes plain and simple: this has nothing to do with the wellbeing of the addict, but how it has been affecting you. Granted, there is usefulness in these declarations which need to be stated. However, the main focus must be on the addict, what the disease has done to him or her, and the future consequences of a choice to continue the addiction versus a choice to accept help. Believe me, if you can get the addict into recovery, you will have your time to address the heartache and torture through which you have been forced. It is an absolutely necessary step in the addict's recovery to address the hurt they have caused. You will have your day. In the meantime, you can share a brief picture of the "hell" their addiction has been causing you, but if dwelled upon, the intervention will go nowhere, fast.

Second, it is human nature to want to simply unload on the addict in an attempt to "wake him up" to his mistakes and path of self-destruction. There will be a desire to use humiliation and shame to try to persuade the addict into looking into a mirror, recognizing their condition, and reaching the epiphany they need to get help. Unfortunately, this works about as well as trying to shame an overweight person into a weight loss program by showing him a self-portrait and telling him how pathetic he looks. Humiliation and shame do not work, and only drives the addict deeper into the pit. You must remember this addiction is where they have found their false comfort and escape, and humiliation and shame will drive them right back to their false chemical security. Successful intervention conversations start with identifying the truth of what the addiction has done to the addict and everyone around him. However, the outcome of the intervention effort must provide the addict with promises of love, support and, most of all, hope!

If you are the addict reading this book, you need to ask yourself just how low you are willing to go. If you are reading this book, it is because you or a loved one is on a downward spiral and even though the addiction is lying to you, you are smart enough to know that you cannot continue doing what you are doing and keep yourself from diving even lower. So what exactly are you willing to lose before you finally admit that you need help? I am not going to lie to you and candy coat anything; it is tough to get through the first few days. Those few days are but a blur in your rearview mirror once you are on your way back to the top.

I believe that the present suffering is nothing compared to the coming glory that is going to be revealed to us. The whole creation waits breathless with anticipation for the revelation of God's sons and daughters.
Romans 8:18-19 (CEB)

For Jerry, the bottom was on that infamous April morning when he arrived at work at his normal time. It was a typical spring day with a campus full of excited students who were all ready for the school year to come to a close. For Jerry, however, this particular April was a special one, as he and his teaching staff were just a few days away from receiving an award of which most school principals can only dream. This award was being bestowed to Jerry and the staff for their achievement of being recognized as an A+ School of Excellence, of which less than one percent of all schools are honored each year. To the average person who is not an educator, the award means very little. However, if it were a professional athletic event, the whole team would be wearing a championship ring, and the city would honor the team with a ticker-tape parade. The entire school district and community were gearing up for the presentation from the state education department, the air was buzzing with excitement, and Jerry was walking on air. The celebration was drawing near, and there was very little time to prepare for the festivity.

He had just reached his office after strolling about the playgrounds and welcoming the students off the morning buses when he received a phone call from the local police department detective. The officer greeted Jerry with the typical friendly formalities and invited him to come down to the station and visit them concerning some recent issues at the school. Assuming he was headed to view some surveillance footage of a weekend trespasser or vandal, Jerry drove down to the station and met the detective at the front door.

As the two sat down and began to talk, they shared a few respectful formalities and brief small talk concerning the recent spring rains and their favorite picks for the beginning of the current professional baseball season. Then, without any warning, Jerry was completely blindsided by the unexpected accusations of his opiate abuse. His mind immediately began racing and scrambling for an escape route of lies or excuses. His heart was pumping through his throat as he held back the overwhelming urge to choke up the little he had for breakfast. As Jerry sat listening to the allegations and formulating his best defense, a sudden but strange sense of relief came over his mind and heart. The overwhelming feeling that overrode all thought and speech was telling him that it was time to quit the lies and games. It was time to stop hiding and time to admit that he had lost total control and had absolutely no more fight left inside. It was the opportunity to finally confess and confront the enemy's death grip.

Jerry soon began to slump from his proud, professional posture and slowly melted into a bent-over and broken man. His crossed leg slowly slipped off his knee and sat flat on the floor. With his chin to his chest and his forehead in his hands, Jerry began to nod his head in agreement with the allegations while he imagined his entire life being ripped out from his hands. Through his own choices and actions, he had given up the right to the woman who held his heart. He had crushed the respect of the two children who were the meaning of his life. He had thrown away a career that cost him and his family years of higher education and countless sacrificed days of dedication to his studies and the job.

The house that he had built with his own two hands was soon to be a place he would only visit instead of live. All of which was given up for a mere chemical substance contained in a tiny white pill.

For the first time in a few years, Jerry was actually thinking straight again. He was seeing the world and reality as he had once seen it through the eyes of innocence, before the addiction began to take control. It all seemed simple now, and so simple that he could not believe he had not seen it heading toward this crash and stopping before it was too late.

As Jerry drove away from the police department that morning in complete silence and without his job, Lucifer was whispering in his ear. Suicide was the most sensible solution in his irrational state of reasoning and, with the correct and precise maneuver in his truck, and at a high enough speed, it could easily be made to appear as an innocent accident. No mess to clean up from a nasty gunshot would be needed, and Maggie and the kids would still benefit from the healthy life insurance policy. Jerry was truly standing on the doorstep of hell and all he had to do was knock. All he had to do was make a split second decision and it could all be over, and the pain gone. Hoping that his tragic death would overshadow his humiliating failure and, therefore, protect his wife and children from having to live under the shadow of his embarrassment, Jerry eyeballed the next oncoming semi-truck and began to cheat over into the wrong lane. He placed his left tires on the double yellow lines and began to pick up speed as he focused in on the ideal impact point. Without second thoughts or any hesitation, Jerry's complete concentration became tunneled on one small speck of paint on the front bumper of the semi-truck and the sound of his winding engine. Suddenly, without any warning, from out of nowhere and without any explanation, beginning to grow from within the deepest core of his heart, an overpowering warming feeling of calm, strength and determination slowly overtook his whole body. It was a euphoric warmth he had never before experienced and one that was not a physical heating. It was a warmth that a newborn baby must feel as he is wrapped tightly in his mother's loving arms for the very first time, giving him an instant and unmistakable sense of peace, and an assurance that everything would be fine. Visions of his children's birth and flashes of their childhood smiles added even more comfort to Jerry's warming heart. While still confused, dazed and trying to make sense of where this supernatural sensation of complete serenity had come from, he blindly drove right past the oncoming semi-truck he had targeted as his life-ending escape. He cannot recall even one minute of the remaining drive to his house nor could he tell you how he even got inside the front door. His next memory was of standing in his empty and quiet home as numbness, uncertainty, and powerlessness flooded back into his bones.

Jerry could think of nothing, but to sit himself at the kitchen table and await Maggie's entrance. In his kindhearted nature, Dr. Robinson, Jerry's boss and friend, had taken the time to sit down with Maggie, prepare her for the earth shattering news, and then sent her home for the remainder of the day. Jerry wasn't sure if Maggie would actually be coming home that day, and he knew very well that she had every justified right and reason to choose otherwise. So when he did hear the front doorknob begin to turn, a small seedling of hope took root deep in his heart. As Maggie walked through the front door, Jerry could not bring himself to lift his head and look her in the eyes. Instead, he stayed seated and stared humbly at the table, knowing that not a word from his mouth could comfort her soul. He had completely broken and destroyed the heart of the very woman that he vowed to love and protect for the rest of his life. He had placed her right in front of the speeding train that he was always supposed to shield her from. No apologies, no promises and no guarantees could ease the emptiness and brokenness that Maggie was feeling at that moment. Her sobs and painful quiet cries were just more indications of the complete state of helplessness into which he had put her. When he finally gathered the courage to lift his head, seeing the tears on her cheeks he had caused was more than his conscience could handle. All he could do was watch as she walked down the hallway to the bedroom and shut the door behind herself.

Throughout the rest of the day, Jerry tried to do as much damage control as possible by sending out text messages and emails to his family members and closest friends. The messages read, "I only send this message to you because I care what you think of me and I respect you enough that I want to be the first to inform you of a recent development. I know I should be calling and talking to you but when the message is complete, you will understand why the embarrassment is simply too much. For a few years now, I have been successfully hiding an addiction to the painkillers that I began taking for my spine. It has reached a point now that I made a terrible choice in my attempts to obtain more pills. The consequences of that decision includes the loss of my job and pending legal matters. I am so sorry that I did not get help before it came to this and I know that my family and I will be paying for this mistake for the rest of our lives. I do eventually want to talk with you and share the details, but right now I ask that you respect the fact that my family needs some alone time to work through the shock."

Of course, there were dozens of replies and incoming calls from the recipients, which Jerry ignored as he sat staring at the kitchen wall. So far, he had seen just a hint of the devastation caused to his wife and sent out quite an impersonal message to a handful of others. However, the hardest part was yet to come, and that was breaking the hearts of his two children, who had placed their dad on the highest and most precious pedestal that could be imagined. Elaine and Allen could not be more proud of who their mother and father had become in the public eye, and the two enjoyed the attention they would get from community members who held their dad on that same pedestal. Elaine and Jerry were closer than your average father-daughter duo. They had been spending nearly every day together for the last six years ever since she was eleven years old and began her quest to earn a Division 1 softball scholarship. Many of their daily hitting and catching workouts ended in high tension between the two, but there had been a bond created that seemed to survive even the harshest of disagreements. Allen and Jerry had the typical father-son relationship, where at the age of twelve, Allen still looked up to and admired his father. They were hunting buddies who shared a passion for the outdoors and loved every second they spent together, whether the hunt was successful or not. They shared much of the same humor, and Allen was beginning to demonstrate many of the traits he had inherited from Jerry.

As the sun set behind the grassy hill to the west of the house, Jerry knew his children would be returning home from their spring athletic practices. His stomach was burning with the anticipation and wishing there was a way to avoid the pain he was about to cause in their hearts. Within minutes, he heard the car doors close and the squeaking of the front gate, as it swung open. The sounds of their laughter and chatting coming up the walkway was an indication that they had not yet gotten wind of or even a hint of the day's disaster.

Elaine was the first to step across the threshold and instantly detected the uneasiness in the air. Being a normal twelve-year-old, Allen's senses were not yet as fine-tuned and he continued to carry on their conversation as he passed right by his sister who stood frozen, and looking at her dad, knowing something was not right. Jerry called everyone to the living room couch and the four sat down as a whole family. He proceeded to tell them that he had been fighting the addiction for a long time and doing the best he could to hide it from them and everyone else in order to spare their embarrassment. However, that plan had backfired and now he wished with all of his heart that he had brought it out into the open long ago. He went on to explain to them that he had been let go from his job and informed them that he would be seeking help to break the addiction and a job outside of the city. As the tears rolled down his children's cheeks, it became obvious to Jerry that holding some of the details back for the time being was probably a smart thing to do. They had enough to try to soak in for one night and adding the fact that their dad would also face legal consequences might just push them over the edge.

They sat for another few minutes just embracing each other in silent tears, nobody knowing what words to say. While sitting and holding each other tightly, for the very first time since their births, Jerry had seen his family for what they truly were. They were an amazing gift from God, to whom he was responsible for guiding, protecting, caring, loving and providing, all of which he had completely failed. At no time should our children ever have to worry about their next meal or how the bills will be paid. Their worries should be on the next baseball game or algebra test. Now, Jerry had placed this dreadful weight of uncertainty on their shoulders, and no promise he could make, or vow he could proclaim would ease their overwhelming sense of helplessness and insecurity.

As would be expected, there was not much sleep to be had that night. Maggie and Jerry rested on their farthest edges of the mattress as if two strangers were forced to share a bed. Afraid that if he was to close his eyes he would awaken to find Maggie gone for good, he laid staring at the faint, dark outline of the ceiling fan and pondering the "what if's" of his choices over the last year. Through the long sleepless hours, Jerry's stomach burned with guilt and regret over every poor decision he had made along the way. Each previous instance where he had passed up a chance to call out for help would flash through his head. Each illustration of remorse tied an even tighter knot in his stomach. As dawn's first light began to peek through the bedroom window, Jerry reluctantly arrived at the conclusion that he indeed had been begging God to break the iron bars of this personal dungeon. If this was The Lord's will and plan for answering that prayer, Jerry had no choice but to accept God's mysterious ways. Without a wink of sleep, Jerry stood up from the bed the next morning and came face to face with the unsureness of any factor of his life. He was forced to come to grips with the reality in what had happened was not just a terrible nightmare from which to awaken, and he was powerless to change what had transpired. The only thing Jerry had any power over was the decision of what to do next, and the attitude and effort he would give to his future plans.

Even though he knew there was no escaping the felony charges against him, Jerry still needed to hire an attorney to help guide him through the hopeless process. Having absolutely no experience in the subject matter, he propped open his laptop and began an internet search for his legal defense. Unsure of what to look for and having no reason to be finicky, he dialed the telephone number for the first name that appeared on the list. He gave a brief description of his situation, and of course, the attorney agreed to take his case and his money, and arranged an emergency conference for that afternoon. Jerry climbed in his truck and drove the two hours to the attorney's office where he fully confessed to everything and expected no mercy. His new representative promised him nothing in exchange for the healthy fee except a good fight for a lenient sentencing. He requested that Jerry immediately enroll in an addiction therapy program in order to improve his chances for lighter punishment. Agreeing that it was more than he deserved, Jerry shook his hand, wrote him a check and returned to his empty house and to his computer to locate his next stop.

Once again, having absolutely no knowledge or experience with addiction counseling, Jerry was content calling the first recovery center that appeared on his computer screen. As the web page began to open, Jerry began to question the purpose or motivation to go to any such counseling. He began reasoning that if losing his job was not enough to make him quit, then no psychologist and group counseling would be able to pull off the miracle. He also concluded that it would not be long before Maggie came to her senses and either moved out or asked him to leave. Finally, whether light or heavy, he was going to pay the legal consequences and have a scar on his record so horrendous that he would never see a steady paycheck again. With the voice in his ear robbing him of any hope, Jerry questioned why he should even make the call. So instead, he jotted the phone number of the facility on a napkin and closed the computer.

The enemy's whispers continued to cut through the silence of the empty house, and as the time for Elaine and Allen to return home from school drew near, Jerry once again began to contemplate the benefits of a well-staged vehicle accident. He knew that Maggie's teacher's salary alone was not going to cover the house, cars, and bills. He could not bear to imagine watching his children leave the home in which they had spent every Christmas since they were born. His two life insurance policies totaled a sum that would be plenty to pay off the house and put some away for the future. He nodded his head in agreement, as the justification echoed through his mind that if the only way he could provide for his children was by being dead, then that is what he must do.

With his keys in his hands, he sat on the couch working out every detail. It was important that it appear that he was driving somewhere and for a purpose. He had one shot at this, and he had to do it right. He could leave nothing to chance and give the insurance company absolutely no reason to deny full payment. After a few more minutes of mentally rehearsing the plan, he was convinced that he had every detail covered and began to type up the text message that would tell Maggie and the children that he was headed out and would return in a couple hours.

Jerry picked up his cell phone and his hands began to tremble as his thumbs proceeded to type the final words that he would say to his family and, therefore, he made sure to end the message with the statement, "I LOVE YOU!!!" With his thumb an inch above the send button, Jerry contemplated whether to leave out the last three words. He wondered if an insurance lawyer would pick up on the hidden meaning and see that there was finality in his message and therefore proof of his premeditation. However, he could not just leave this world and his family behind without some sort of closure or expressing how he truly felt. He sat trying to decide whether to send the message or change it, and just as he had made the choice and reached for the send button, the doorbell startled Jerry right out of his seat. That made him lose his grip on the phone, throwing it half way across the room and under the sofa.

He stood a few feet from the front door fighting with himself over the decision to open it or ignore the visitor. The doorbell rang again and was followed up by a sturdy knock. Taking in a deep sigh and rolling his eyes at the interruption of his plans, Jerry opened the door and found his former coaching partner standing on his porch. The two had always been close. Jerry had a lot of respect for Mr. Mendez, so he invited him in and offered him a seat. Coach Mendez was a spiritual man who was not ashamed of his belief in Christ and was not shy to share the story of the Gospel. Jerry opened up to his friend and shared some of the details of the battle he had been fighting over the past couple of years, but made sure to end the testimony with a statement assuring Mr. Mendez that he and his family would recover and be fine. The coach nodded his head as he listened and then asked permission to pray with Jerry. Jerry agreed, bowed his head and listened to the words of care, compassion and hope that poured from his heart. After ending the prayer, he handed Jerry a pamphlet and asked him to consider the addiction facility, as it was the same facility that his nephew had attended and returned home a changed man. Jerry took the pamphlet, shook his hand, and thanked him for stopping by. After his friend had shut the door on his way out, without even glancing at it, Jerry tossed the brochure next to his computer and walked over to pick his phone off the living room floor.

Just as Jerry stooped for the phone, the front door opened again. Allen had returned from baseball practice and Elaine was right behind him. Without saying a word, Allen walked over and hugged his dad tightly, holding on to him a little longer than the usual embrace between the two. Elaine chose to use her words and asked Jerry how he was doing, but did not delve into any details. By their demeanor and the looks on their faces, it was obvious they had been bombarded with questions throughout the day from schoolmates and teachers. As he stood staring and watching the two walk down the hallway towards their bedrooms, Jerry tried to imagine the humiliation they had been put through and would continue to suffer for months to come. He thought about just how alone and deserted they had to have felt as they walked among the eight hundred students on campus. Jerry started to head for their rooms while trying to think of something he could say that might ease their pain even a little. However, by the time he reached their bedroom doors, all he could do is stand and watch as they removed the schoolbooks from their bags in preparation to start their homework assignments. Once again, he concluded the obvious, that nothing he could say would ease any of the pain and helplessness they were feeling. At that point, his words were about as worthless as a chewed piece of gum on the bottom of a shoe.

Jerry decided to abandon his plans for the night and try again the next day. It wasn't like he had a lot of things on his agenda, and he figured it would be easier to sell a daytime trip out of town than the late evening trip he was preparing to take. He turned on his phone, erased the text that he had prepared to send, and figured he would compose another one the next day. After discarding the message, he noticed an unread message from Maggie's brother, John. Not knowing what to expect from the protective sibling, he hesitantly opened the text and read the message. John explained that he had heard the troubling news and wanted to reach out and offer Jerry the chance to work. John was a business owner who was in need of filling an entry-level labor position that could not come close to paying what Jerry had been earning, but would at least provide him with some income and the ability to supplement Maggie's paycheck. John and his family lived about a four-hour drive from Jerry's house, so he also offered the charity of a free room, food and caring companionship while working for him and getting back on his feet.

Jerry still had every intention of carrying out his plan to ensure his family would collect his life insurance, but figured he had better agree to the offer so as to not raise a red flag signaling that he had lost all hope and surrendered the will to go on. He replied to the text thanking him and assuring John that he would call soon to plan the details of his move.

Even though all four members of the family were in the house later that evening, it almost seemed to be abandoned, empty and silent. With everyone walking around in a complete fog and numbness, nothing but the occasional small talk was uttered, and not even a "goodnight" was spoken as the lights turned off one by one throughout the late evening hours. Once again, Jerry and Maggie stretched out on their opposite sides of the bed, and he laid on his side looking at the back of his wife who silently cried herself to a few minutes of sleep for a second night in a row.

Jerry's exhaustion did cause him to fall asleep for about an hour, only to be awakened by a nightmare that included a vision of his two children's headstones next to his own freshly buried grave. After seeing that haunting image in his dreams, he was unable to close his eyes again, so he walked himself out to the living room couch where the nightmare repeatedly replayed in his head. Jerry started to ask himself if it was just a screwed up dream caused by the stress and complete lack of sleep, a hallucination brought on by withdrawal, or if it was something else trying to get through. He began to question if the dream was supposed to have any meaning or message to it whatsoever, then what could it be. The first and only conclusion at which he could arrive was maybe his death would also be the cause of the complete destruction of his children as well. Just the thought of that possibility pulled Jerry out of his selfish bubble of pity for just a second. That is all it took for him to realize what the true outcome would be as a result of taking his own life. Starting to regain some of his rational thinking abilities, Jerry acknowledged the need to take responsibility, be the man he had been expected to be, dedicate himself to an addiction recovery effort and, whether it was living under the same roof as his family or separated, he needed to give Maggie and his children the very best support he could provide.

Once he had arrived at the final decision to move forward with the idea of getting help for his addiction, he recalled receiving a text from his mom on the previous day. Upon receipt of the message and realizing the content of the text, he disregarded it and closed his phone. Jerry had ignored her numerous attempts to contact him by phone and finally replied to her through a text stating that he was ok and would call her soon. She returned a message that suggested a specific addiction-counseling center. Jerry, very skeptical but now actually having a reason to view the entire text, reopened it up and began reading the message. His mom stated that while worrying about her youngest son and in her struggles to sleep, she began to pray to The Lord and asked for His wisdom and guidance to heal Jerry of his disease, salvage his marriage, and to provide the daily needs of the family. Soon after her prayer, it began weighing heavily on her heart to recommend that Jerry consider calling the "Calvary Addiction Recovery Center." She went on to tell Jerry that she felt it was a message that The Lord wanted her to pass on and so she did.

Jerry cynically snickered at his mom's message as he closed his phone and leaned his head back against the sofa. He sat for the next few minutes contemplating the idea of attending addiction counseling and wondering how it would be possible while also trying to earn some desperately needed money. The more he thought about it and fretted over the struggles that were ahead, his anxiety began to stir up an uneasiness in his stomach. Finally reaching the point of complete hopelessness again, he reluctantly surrendered to the fact that he indeed needed to commit to his recovery and would figure out the logistics later. Jerry returned to his laptop and flipped over the napkin on which he had written the number of a counseling center. He struck a button on the laptop keyboard to awaken it from its dormant mode and watched the screen slowly start to brighten. To his chilling and bewildered disbelief, the words that began to take shape from the dark screen read, "Calvary Addiction Recovery Center." It was the same name that his mom had texted the day before. Still in astonishment, Jerry then reached across the table and flipped over the brochure that Coach Mendez had provided, and the goose bumps instantly caused every hair on his body to stand at attention. There on the table and staring directly at him was the pamphlet matching his mom's text message, his computer screen, and the number written on the napkin. Accepting that this was a little more than a mere coincidence, Jerry returned to the laptop screen and jotted down the location of the center. Once again, causing Jerry to recognize the absolute unlikelihood of such a random chance, he could do nothing but shake his head in disbelief that the center was also conveniently located as the closest facility to John's house in the city. With this latest fact at hand, all skepticism and cynical thoughts left his mind, and there became no doubt as to where Jerry would call to request help.

Jerry felt it was important that Maggie be involved in the decision, so waited for her return from work before calling Calvary. Maggie's interest level was not that of the greatest enthusiasm, but she did exhibit a small sign of interest in the quality and success rate of the facility. It did not matter the reason that she cared, what mattered to Jerry is that she did, and that fact added some water to his seed of hope. As they spoke with a representative on the phone, it was apparent that they had chosen a quality recovery center, which was also based on Biblical principles and Christian beliefs. They had also informed him of the opportunity to enroll as an outpatient allowing him to work while attending the facility. With these facts in hand and all that had unfolded throughout the day, Jerry was finally ready to begin his program. However, since Jerry was scheduled to attend his first court appearance in less than a week, he had to postpone his inaugural day, but was able to set an appointment and reserve his seat at the treatment center.

Jerry still had a week to burn before starting his treatment classes, and in the meantime, more and more friends and family members called and visited Jerry, pledging their support and offering comfort through their empathy, understanding and forgiveness. With each visitor and conversation, the absolute bleakness started to fade little by little and was replaced by a few more seeds of hope. However, it was his appointment with the ruthless prosecuting attorney, though, that left Jerry completely speechless and sent him right to his knees.

The anticipation of his arraignment hearing ate at Jerry's stomach and caused countless hours of staring at the ceiling fan while everyone else in the house was asleep. Jerry's courtroom experience was no more than watching a few television dramas and a one-day call to jury duty, which was canceled as soon as he arrived. He had no clue of what to expect and had not heard a word from his lawyer. Dressed in his best shirt and tie, Jerry drove to the courthouse and walked to the waiting area to be called in when it was his turn.

It became pretty obvious to Jerry that for the purpose of complete humiliation, the waiting area had absolutely no privacy or confidentiality, as it was strategically placed front and center in the corridor where everyone must walk past in order to get anywhere in the county courthouse building. Needless to say, while sitting for what seemed the entire morning, Jerry saw numerous acquaintances pass through the hallways. Even though they tried to spare Jerry the embarrassment and pretended as if they did not notice him sitting in the hot seat, he knew there was no missing his presence, and the humiliation that he had caused all on his own, continued to pile on his shoulders.

With only a minute to spare, Jerry's attorney arrived out of breath and said nothing except an order to Jerry to let him do the speaking. A few seconds later, another individual who Jerry would consider a family friend, came out of the courthouse doors and called Jerry into the room. As the judge's entrance was announced, Jerry recognized the robed man as the father of three former students and basketball players, whom Jerry had once coached. Jerry recalled several instances when the dad had commended him for his coaching abilities and his gift for teaching children. Now, the same man was about to list the numerous charges against Jerry and place him in the arena for the prosecuting attorneys to release the lions.

Immediately following his preliminary hearing where Jerry heard the felony charges against him, he and his defense lawyer, who definitely had not earned one penny of the steep fee that he was charging, were called to the prosecutor's office to meet with the District Attorney and the elected Sheriff. Now, Jerry had grown up a big Eastwood fan and had memorized almost every line that Clint ever uttered in his movies.

This particular real-life enforcement duo with whom Jerry was meeting had been rumored to be no different from the film characters of Marshal Jed Cooper and Judge Fenton, who in "Hang 'Em High", sent every man to the gallows to pay with their lives for their crimes. As Jerry accepted the invitation to sit in a chair across the table from the ruthless partners, the first words from District Attorney Thompson confirmed those nasty rumors. He set his elbows on the table, placed a fist inside the other hand, leaned towards Jerry and bluntly explained that in his long career of prosecuting criminal cases, he had a zero percent history of pursuing anything less than the maximum sentences. D.A. Thompson clarified that he slept very well every night knowing that he was consistent and consequently, never felt any guilt for playing favorites or allowing his emotions to override the written law.

Understanding and accepting this declaration, Jerry bowed his closed eyes towards the table, took a deep breath, then lifted his head to face and accept the consequences he had brought upon himself and that he fully deserved. Jerry's heart began to pump through his throat and his hands shook uncontrollably as he waited for the hammer to drop. Haunting visions of the unbearable humiliation that would be brought on Elaine and Allen as children of an imprisoned convict induced a physical sickness surging up inside Jerry's stomach. Imagining the unstable and tormented life that would be inflicted on Maggie caused the room to begin spinning in his head and brought Jerry to the brink of unconsciousness.

"However," Mr. Thompson stated as he lifted his elbows, folded his arms across his chest, and leaned back in his chair. "God told me that there will always be a first, and I guess this case is it."

Jerry's eyes widened with a glimmer of hope, he straightened his shoulders and listened for the rest. D.A. Thompson went on to explain that out of numerous other possible prosecuting attorneys with much lighter caseloads, Jerry's case file somehow still managed to land on his desk, and ever since, had weighed heavily on his heart. Never before feeling or experiencing such a burden, and losing sleep over a cut and dry case, he resorted to prayer and asked God for clarification. He paused for a few seconds and then quoted a scripture from the book of Romans.

God works all things together for good for the ones who love God, for those who are called according to his purpose.

"I don't know what He has in mind Jerry, but The Lord has plans for you, and you can't accomplish them with these charges on your record." He paused again as he stared into Jerry's eyes and then announced that upon the successful completion of rehabilitation treatment and proof of a year of addiction recovery, the prosecution team was committed to drop and erase all charges, and his record would be completely expunged.

Stay at the Bottom or Start Climbing: It's Your Choice

With his defense lawyer just as stunned as he was, Jerry was speechless, could only shake Mr. Thompson's hand vowing not to disappoint him, and walked out of the courthouse in complete shock. The emotional high-speed rollercoaster had simply been too much for Jerry over the last week and when he climbed into his truck, the welled-up pressure was too great to hold back any longer and the floodgates flew open. For the first time since he had been dismissed from his principal's duties, his emotions were finally given a crack in the door from which to escape, and there was no stopping what he had been holding inside. Tears of disappointment, sorrow, guilt, hopelessness as well as cries of joy and relief were all shed inside that soundproof pickup cab. He is not sure how long he sat hunched over in the driver's seat that afternoon, but after exhausting all his energy and hydration to the uncontrollable outburst of tears, he collected himself and found a renewed courage welling up from his soul. There was light in the distance that he could see. He didn't know exactly what it was or where it was taking him, but it was undeniably God's light, and refusing to follow it is what got him in this situation in the first place.

Later that afternoon, Jerry shared the legal decisions with Maggie as she sat emotionlessly watching him pack his suitcase. He loaded some carpenter tools in his truck, hugged his very distant wife, kissed his teary-eyed children and started on his four-hour drive to his new job and the treatment center. Along the lonely and dark desert road, he had plenty of time to reflect on all that had transpired. His emotions bounced from one extreme to the other as he questioned his unclear future. He was still in a state of shock over the demonstration of God's grace and mercy that had been displayed at the courthouse. Yet he wondered if he would still have a wife and children when he returned. If God does have a purpose for him, how could He possibly use a person with such a broken past? Would any employer ever trust him to serve in any position of leadership or value? Would he ever again be looked at with respect and dignity, as he once was through the eyes of parents and students alike?

From one thought to another, his mind bounced like a ping-pong ball; from Maggie to his children, from bills to bankruptcy, and from the most confident visions of total redemption, to utter failure and desperation. He soon began to fixate on the addiction facility and the uncertainty of what embarrassing and humiliating confessions he would be required to share in front of complete strangers. Part of him felt excited that he could finally face the demon that had tormented him for so long and had taken control over his life. Oddly enough, he enjoyed a sense of relief that he no longer had to hide, but was also completely disgraced that it was exposed to all and now known by everyone. As he reached the second and third hour of the drive, his old and prejudiced views of addiction began to creep back into his mind as he pictured the treatment center and imagined himself in a room full of strung-out, half-dead teenagers whose only problems were not knowing how and when to stop partying. He was convinced that he would be spending the next four months amongst a group of immature young adults who could not relate to his situation, and who would laugh and mock the "old man" that just couldn't say no to some pills.

He arrived late that night at his brother-in-law's house, humbly accepted the bedroom that John and his wife had prepared, and thanked them for their gracious acceptance of him into their home. He shut the bedroom door, set his bags and work boots on the floor, and stood staring at the walls and the neatly made bed. Realizing that this was now his new home and life, he whispered under his breath, "God, what have I done?"

Jerry didn't even crawl under the covers that night nor did he comfort his head on a pillow. There is a distinct and recognizable level of "low" to which only a husband and father who has walked in these shoes can bear witness. It was a feeling of being completely undeserving of any forgiveness, compassion, favor or comfort. He didn't want any of these, and actually was overcome by complete guilt when he considered accepting any form of mercy, including what was offered to him earlier that day in the courtroom. The accumulated weight of every child he had callously persecuted when he was serving as a teacher and principal for so many years, was sitting on his shoulders, and he was waiting for his own punishment to be handed down. Yet, it seemed at every corner he turned, clemency and kindness were waiting for him, which was even more torturous to his guilt-ridden and shattered pride.

With little more than an hour of broken sleep, Jerry rose out of bed to his alarm clock and set out to find the home and people in which he had placed his trust and hope of conquering his vice. It took him a few missed streets and U-turns, but he finally arrived at the quaint set of buildings laid out amongst a few plush lawns and park benches. The bright-eyed receptionist took all of his information without once losing her smile and cheery voice, which was reassuring in some manners. However, the sense of security that she radiated was overshadowed by his self-torment and thoughts that if the woman knew even the slightest details of his failures, she would not have been so welcoming. She described what the next four months would entail and, of course, arranged Jerry's monthly payments. He looked over his new daily schedule and signed a few papers. It was final; he was checked in to begin his road to recovery.

Like a freshman walking his new high school grounds for the first time, Jerry stared at his campus map and surveyed the buildings and doors in attempts to locate his first session. Not only was he walking into one of the most uncomfortable situations of his life, but he was also arriving a few minutes late, which put him front and center for his awkward grand entrance. After a few minutes of searching his surroundings, he finally located the correct room, right where the receptionist had told him it would be. Jerry grabbed the door handle, took a deep breath, and gave it a tug. As the door opened, he began to hear the sounds of music, cheerful conversation and unexpected laughter from the other side. He hesitated to walk in and instead, peeked his head around the corner, immediately determining he was in the wrong building. The room was full of well-dressed and finely groomed adults, drinking coffee and mingling. One of the older men invited him in, asked to see Jerry's schedule, and upon a quick glance, welcomed him to the group. He informed Jerry that they were just about to start and for him to pour a cup of coffee and to grab a seat and make himself at home. Confused and trying to figure out who all of these wealthily garbed people might be, Jerry timidly walked into the room and chose one of the twenty vacant chairs that had been arranged in a large circle. As soon as the music stopped, without any spoken direction, the crowd dispersed to the seats and began to settle in. Once the last person had sat down, the same older gentleman who welcomed Jerry at the door, took control of the group by leading in a prayer and stating the activities planned for the day. He needed no introduction for Jerry to understand that he was the facilitating counselor and was in charge of the room. He introduced himself as James Corbett, and welcomed Jerry as the newest member to the team. He explained that Jerry would soon get a chance to share his story and his purpose for attending, but first, would allow the rest of the class to introduce themselves to Jerry and share a brief portion of theirs.

Jerry's heart began to pump up into his throat once again and he glanced at the doorway, wondering if he could make it out before being tackled. He absolutely did not want to share any of his pathetic confession of failure, and especially now that he would be sharing it with such professional and dignified adults. He began to organize his thoughts and compose the kind of story that he used to tell as a kid; a story that wasn't necessarily a lie, but one that didn't exactly divulge the whole truth. The testimony of the first two participants were simply mumbles in Jerry's ears as he pretended to listen, but instead, was formulating his story. As the next participant began to speak, Jerry's mind completely froze as his attention was grabbed by the voice of a broken woman spilling her soul to the group. She was a medical doctor who, knowing too well the dangers of prescription pain medications, still became addicted while dealing with a chronic knee injury. She had since lost her license to practice medicine and was trying to find the path for the rest of her career and life. Jerry had to force his mouth shut as it hung open in complete surprise, and the shocking testimonies did not end there. The next was a college athletic coach who resorted to heroin once his doctor would no longer prescribe the medications for a back injury. However, the story wasn't over, as he went on to explain that he used a couple of players as his mules; who, in trade for more playing time, would buy the drug off the street and bring it to their coach. Then it was the businesswoman who, after undergoing a hysterectomy, drained her corporate account while illegally purchasing opiates from street vendors. There were police officers, lawyers, and waitresses, all alike, and all sharing the same story of demise. By the time it was Jerry's turn to speak, he realized he was just one of thousands affected by this horrible illness, and not the "lone loser" he had considered himself. Jerry shared every last bit of his story that morning and hid not one detail from the group. Each member nodded in empathy to the all-too-well-known screenplay he described, and gave him the comforting promise, "This too shall pass."

At the closing of his story, Jerry shared with the group that his biggest fear of all was never again being able to redeem himself and unable to be that husband, dad and leader that everyone once saw as their "knight in shining armor." Mr. Corbett snickered under his breath, stated the irony of Jerry's statement, and explained how it served as a perfect transition into his opening scripture of the day. He grabbed the bookmark from his Bible, forced the pages open to where it had been wedged, and began to read.

We were saved in hope. If we see what we hope for, that isn't hope. Who hopes for what they already see? But if we hope for what we don't see, we wait for it with patience.

In the same way, the Spirit comes to help our weakness. We don't know what we should pray, but the Spirit himself pleads our case with unexpressed groans. The one who searches hearts knows how the Spirit thinks, because he pleads for the saints, consistent with God's will. We know that God works all things together for good for the ones who love God, for those who are called according to his purpose. We know this because God knew them in advance, and he decided in advance that they would be conformed to the image of his Son. That way his Son would be the first of many brothers and sisters. Those who God decided in advance would be conformed to his Son, he also called. Those whom he called, he also made righteous. Those whom he made righteous, he also glorified.

> *So what are we going to say about these things? If God is for us, who is against us? He didn't spare his own Son but gave him up for us all. Won't he also freely give us all things with him?*
>
> Romans 8: 24-32 (CEB)

Up to now, there had been a few "hair- raising" coincidences that made Jerry pause and ponder the possibility of divine intervention. He had an overwhelming, and almost a possessive overtaking of his body and mind that caused him to miss his perfectly timed head-on collision with the oncoming semi-truck. His long-time coaching friend interrupted the sending of his well thought-out text message to his family and then kept him home long enough for his family to return home. He had a dream that forced him to reconsider his selfish solution to the whole problem. His mother, who lived hundreds of miles away, sends a random message recommending a specific treatment center, out of dozens to choose from, that is then backed up by two other unrelated sources. However, out of all of the verses that could have been chosen on Jerry's first day, the exact same verse quoted by the district attorney was planned months in advance by Mr. Corbett to be the topic of discussion for the day.

As he closed his Bible, Mr. Corbett expressed to Jerry that indeed he would never be able to wear his "shining armor" again. However, the most respected and honored knights of the land are those with scuffed, damaged and dented armor, for they are the knights who are chosen to lead others through battles.

Jerry sat in complete humbleness and began to open his eyes to a new reality that he had never noticed before. It was the reality that his pride and reasoning had never allowed him to see. Indeed, God is in control of everything, and we simply have a choice as to how we react, respond and move forward. He began to think even deeper and asked himself how he had even ended up in the successful position of a husband, father, and school principal. He reasoned that it was due to his intelligence, which he then admitted was a gift from God. It was due to his ability to use common sense, which is a gift from God, which we often wish others had as well. It was a result of his ability to talk with people and form bonds between parents and teachers, which was a gift from God. It was because of his skills to reason and think through conflicts and arrive at a peaceful resolution, which was a gift from God. It was due to his work ethic and willingness to arrive early, stay late and labor on weekends, which was a trait he possessed since he was a child and was also a gift from God. So, what did Jerry actually contribute to earn his success? In all reality, absolutely nothing. He was simply a vessel in which

God planted a combination of skills and abilities to carry out His plan. The responsibility we have is to realize these blessings and allow God to use them. If we choose not to, and choose to use them for our own glory, riches and fortune, then we have denied our Father and have chosen the wide path to destruction and will live and die with the consequences.

By the end of the brief epiphany happening in Jerry's heart, he recognized the fact that if God wants him back in a position of leadership and back in the seat as head of household, then that is where God will put him. Jerry never did have control of what God blessed him with nor did he ever have power over the decisions of those who gave Jerry his promotions and favors. Every bit of it came directly from God and will continue to come from God according to His plan, not ours.

Many plans are in a person's mind, but the LORD's purpose will succeed.
Proverbs 19:21, (CEB)

The remainder of the day in class was spent reviewing human brain functions and the causes of addiction, as well as understanding their own brains and how the disease takes complete control of inhibitions and common sense. Not that Jerry wanted some excuse for his choices and behavior, but the enlightening information helped him grasp and understand many of his past actions that were so foreign to his true nature. Before he knew it, the sun was casting its afternoon shadows, and it was time for Jerry to break from class and take his tools to work.

For the first time in years, besides mowing the lawn, Jerry experienced the reward of some physical labor. Even though it felt good to use some muscle and create with his hands again, Jerry struggled to sit straight at the dinner table that evening with aches and soreness coming from places in his body that he forgot he had. After finishing his dinner prepared by John's wife and helping to clear the table, he retired to his room for the evening. That night, knowing that he was not alone in his battle, Jerry still did not fold back the blankets, but did give his head a pillow.

During the second day of class, Mr. Corbett informed Jerry that he would be required to attend at least three addiction group meetings per week. These could be such groups as Alcoholics Anonymous, Narcotics Anonymous, or any related type meetings. Jerry immediately asked for a variance to such a requirement and explained that this would cause him to miss afternoons of work, and a large sum of income that was needed to support his family. Mr. Corbett silently stared at Jerry, causing an awkward discomfort in the air. After what seemed to be an eternity of angered silence, he authoritatively asked Jerry to list the top three things that were most important and valued in his life. Jerry paused and thought for a few seconds and then stated that first was his family, second would be to rebuild his career, and third would be his outdoor hobbies that he returns to once a year as a reward for his hard work. Mr. Corbett nodded his head in agreement and plainly stated, "If you are not going to put your addiction recovery first place in your life, you will surely lose all three of those things. So now how important are those few hours of work you will miss?"

If Jerry had a tail, it would have been tucked between his legs as he walked back to his seat in the group. The words echoed in his head over the rest of the afternoon and by the end of the second day, Jerry understood and accepted the fact that if he did not get this addiction under control, he indeed would have no chance to reclaim or regain everything he stood to lose. Needless to say, he sat down that evening and searched the internet for local AA and NA meeting locations and times. He found a couple that were friendly to his work schedule and one that cut into a small portion of his earning power, but jotted them down on his calendar and crawled back on top of the neatly made bed.

It had been several weeks since Jerry could remember a night of sleep that lasted longer than an hour or two, and as the anxiety of the family bills, his children's daily struggles at school, Maggie's instantaneous adoption of all household responsibilities, and his inability to fix it anytime in the near future, he had come to the conclusion that this night would be no different. As the minutes on the digital clock continued to tick away and Jerry laid thinking about everything that had been said in the class, he recalled the verses quoted from Romans by the district attorney and repeated by Mr. Corbett. Pondering the coincidence, Jerry turned on the bedside lamp, reached into the nightstand and opened the Bible to those pages once again. He read the chapter in its entirety and placed the Bible back on his chest, looked up at the ceiling and, for the first time in months, began to talk to his Father.

"Ok LORD, if this is Your message and promise to me, then I must surrender it to You, because I do not see any way possible for me to dig out of this hole. Therefore, I give it to You LORD and from this point on; will trust You and Your promise".

Jerry intended to continue his prayer to ask for The Lord's hedge of protection to be placed around his family. He had planned to thank God for everyone who had reached out to help him and his family, and for the grace that had been given to him in the form of a job and the mercy shown by the prosecuting attorney. However, as soon as he had stated his final sentence giving his trust and faith to The Lord, Jerry instantly fell into a sleep that he had not experienced in years.

Don't be anxious about anything; rather, bring up all of your requests to God in your prayers and petitions, along with giving thanks. Then the peace of God that exceeds all understanding will keep your hearts and minds safe in Christ Jesus.

Philippians 4: 6-7 (CEB)

As the early morning alarm clock began to squeak out its annoying screeching beeps; Jerry opened his eyes to find the lamp still on and both hands still on the Bible that laid across his chest. He rose that morning with a renewed sense of hope that he could not completely identify or even start to explain. It was a feeling as if he had been told some great, stress-relieving news, but could not recall what that news might have been. He quietly climbed in the shower as to not awaken the rest of the house, put on his clothes and headed out the door on his way to class. During his drive through the city, he heard the single ring on his cellphone that indicated a text message had been received. Figuring that is was a message from John telling him where to meet for work after class, Jerry left the phone in the cup holder and finished his drive. While exiting the truck and beginning his walk towards the meeting room, he glanced down at his phone screen and the message stopped him in his tracks and brought a euphoric high that no drug could ever match. It was a text from Maggie that simply stated, "Good morning. Hope you have a good day."

LANIER T. NORTHRUP

The First Steps

In class that day, the discussion was focused on steps eight and nine of the Twelve Step Program. For Jerry, it was a foreign language, so he simply sat back and listened to the few classmates who had successfully passed the steps or were currently completing them. As they shared their stories of how fearful they were to begin making amends with those whom they had offended, but how freeing it was once they did, Jerry began to make a mental list of just how many people he had hurt over the years. Of course, the list started with Maggie, Elaine and Allen, and then expanded out to all family members, friends, and coworkers who had placed their trust in his ability and his integrity. He imagined what the conversation would look and sound like and how the individuals might react. He knew some would be more forgiving than others but figured he had the courage to face them all at one time or another. However, it was at the mentioning of one requirement that stopped Jerry in mid- thought and was a step that he was not sure if he would ever be willing to take.

Just as the conversation was coming to a close, Mr. Corbett reminded the class that the completion of steps eight and nine is a huge hurdle and one that does help clear our conscience. However, the steps do us no good if we are not willing to forgive ourselves.

Upon the mentioning of that requirement, Jerry knew he would be hung up on that rung of the ladder for a long time, if not for the rest of his life. At this point Jerry could not ever see a way to forgive himself for what he had caused to everyone he loved. To Jerry, forgiving himself was nothing less than claiming that his choices that cut so many deep wounds into other's hearts was excusable and justifiable. For him, it was just the opposite. Jerry would always hate that man he had become and the man who destroyed his character and integrity.

The more he sat and thought about it, the more confused and angry he became with himself. There was a side of Jerry that was thankful for the acts of mercy that were being extended to him from all directions. On the other hand, he felt there was a penance that needed to be paid, and it needed to be just as hurtful or more painful than what he had caused everyone else. He wanted this punishment. He invited this severe payment of retribution, and the longer he went without it, the more the guilt built up inside.

Mr. Corbett could read Jerry like a book as he blankly stared through the walls and his jaw muscles flinched as he gritted his teeth in disgust with himself. James called out Jerry's name and then repeated it twice again, and each time with a little more volume. With a snap of his head, Jerry came out of his trance and apologized for his lack of attention. Mr. Corbett reminded him that it was the night for Jerry to choose his sponsor at his meetings. Still settling down from the wave of self-rage from which he had just been awoken, he nodded his head in agreement but had truly no idea of what he was speaking.

After being dismissed from class, Jerry drove straight to the address of the little church where he had located his first Narcotics Anonymous meeting. Once again, expecting a slew of strung-out, bar-fighting, bike-riding, purse-snatching roughnecks, Jerry's assumption was again incorrect. Sure, there were a few loud motorcycles and some not-so-kind looking individuals who walked into the basement of the church. However, every one of them had the empathy of a nun and welcomed Jerry as an instant member of a special family. Of course, the setting was a little less organized than the recovery center, but the genuine sincerity of everyone in the room was unmatched.

As the new kid on the block, Jerry was invited to stand and give a brief reason for attending. He gave the condensed version, but also took the opportunity to state his mission for the night and explain that he was in need of a sponsor. At the end of his adlibbed speech, the group applauded and welcomed Jerry to the crowd of misfits, as they called themselves. He took his seat and arrived at the conclusion that there were no takers on his invitation to become his sponsor. The meeting agenda consisted of a few traditional readings, an excerpt from the book *Just for Today*, and some testimonies from a few long-time members and a couple of newcomers. After a half hour had passed, the facilitator called for a short coffee and bathroom break. Jerry started to make his way towards the soda machine where he was intercepted by the man who would become his closest friend over the next few months. He was quite the intimidating man, standing a few inches over six feet, heavier built with a greying short goatee and a few remaining white hairs left on his head. Dressed in a high dollar business suit and smelling of money, he introduced himself as Patrick and asked Jerry to explain the real reason he was there. Feeling as if he was being accused of infiltrating a secret society, Jerry took a step back and asked Patrick what he had meant. Patrick repeated the question and then explained that he wanted to know what Jerry was truly hoping for as an outcome of working through the twelve steps with a sponsor. Jerry thought for a few seconds and then spilled his soul. Jerry explained that he knew that his words would never hold the value that they once held with Maggie, his children and his friends. He was well aware that nothing he could promise would ever convince anyone that Jerry, the addict, would not ever raise his evil head again. The only way he could ever be able to earn back any respect or confidence would be through his actions and would likely take years of these actions to begin earning even the slightest bit of trust. Patrick nodded his head, placed his hand on Jerry's shoulder and explained that if Jerry would have him, he would be honored to be his sponsor.

The two exchanged phone numbers, set a date, time and coffee shop location for their first meeting, shook hands and retreated to their seats for the remainder of the meeting. Jerry was always gifted in the observance of details and one of the promising and encouraging specifics that he noticed about Patrick was the fact that he wore a wedding band. For Jerry, it meant that there was hope for Maggie and him, for if many of these men were attending the meeting and were still married, then maybe Jerry and Maggie could also find a way.

Later that night after returning from his meeting, Jerry joined John and his family at the dinner table and found it in himself to relax a little and join in on some evening discussion. It was also the first meal that Jerry could tell you that he remembered eating and what food was on his plate. Before this time, it had just been a blur of nerves, anxiety, shame and regret. Although the guilt and embarrassment were still unbearable, he felt a little weight off his shoulders. When he retired to his room, he saw absolutely no reason to change the routine that had seemed to start this upward trend. Jerry crawled on top of the neatly made blankets, propped an extra pillow under his head in order to be in better position to read, and decided to start the night from the beginning of the New Testament.

Jerry was able to get through a few chapters of Matthew before unknowingly falling off into another deep sleep. He had made it through the detailed account of Christ's humble birth and into his early days of his ministry, miracles and challenging the Pharisees. However, it was Jesus' constant mentioning of His purpose to replace the Law with Grace that seemed to resonate in Jerry's conscience. He had been raised in a Christian home and even to the extent that his mother led the Sunday morning singing of the hymns and made sure Jerry and his brothers and sister were at every service.

However, he had never read any more of the Bible than what the preacher had read to them in church. He knew the major stories of Christ's birth, miracles and death on the cross. Even though he did not fully comprehend the full meaning or the relationship between the crucifixion and the forgiveness of our sins, he understood it enough to accept the preacher's invitation, and as a ten-year-old boy, walked down the aisle to accept Jesus Christ as his Lord and Savior.

As much as he would like to say that from that point on he always made the right choices and lived the life of a saint, we all know it was not so. There was indeed a difference in his heart, and he definitely could not ignore the new voice in his conscience that subtly reminded him of right and wrong. However, he was still a young boy doing what most every adolescent did in church as he pretended to listen to the message but daydreamed of the plans that were made immediately following the service. Occasionally, he might catch a few words that would convict his heart of some poor choices he had been making and would cause him to rethink his actions. In general, the fundamentals of the "religion" were great guidelines by which to live, and he never took it much farther or deeper than that. To Jerry, God was the infinite being who created everything and, when catching you sinning, would employ an arrangement of punishments that ranged from simply making you feel bad, all the way to shutting the door behind you as he tossed you in the fires of hell. Unless you were quick to plead for forgiveness, it was typically too late and either the punishment was on its way or God would ignore you for an undetermined amount of time. He understood Jesus to be the Son of God and who The Father sent down to earth in order to die so that, even with our sins, we could still make it to Heaven, if those sins were not too bad, and if we did enough good to offset the bad.

As Jerry got older and began his educational career, he started to realize that The Lord was a little closer than simply sitting on his throne in the clouds and throwing lightning bolts at everyone who made mistakes. He found that his prayers were usually answered in some fashion or another, if they were made with the purpose other than selfish motives. He also discovered that God prefers to use a loving method of discipline, but will resort to the level needed to get our attention. Through these few years of becoming a little more acquainted with who God is, Jerry also read a little more of the Bible. However, it was more for the purpose of finding an answer to an immediate pressing issue rather than for an honest understanding of the entire story of the Gospel. Jerry felt that there was no better time than the present to begin reading from Matthew to Revelations and see what God would reveal to him.

Over the next few days, Jerry attended the daily recovery classes and each day, walked away with a very valuable tool to use in his fight against a future relapse. He spent the afternoons swinging a hammer, toting lumber, and sweeping sawdust beneath the floodlights. Moreover, each night after dinner, he would retire to the room, lay on top of the blankets and read as far as his consciousness would allow before falling into another night of deep sleep.

After reading the first two books of the New Testament, Jerry was able to compare Matthew and Mark's accounts of Jesus' life and the passion with which He took to the cross. For the first time, Jerry was comprehending why it had to be Jesus and why He had to suffer and die in the manner in which He did. In order for the sacrifice to satisfy God's requirements, the sinless Son of God and Son of Man had to take the full punishment, forsaking, and death that we all deserved so that no longer would we be held under a law that was impossible to uphold. Once we realize that we cannot follow the law, we turn to our only hope and that is in Christ, surrendering ourselves to him for paying our debt. What Jerry could not understand is why.

Why would God allow this to happen to His Son in order to pay the ransom for a world full of mean, selfish, and hateful people who turn their back on their own creator and trample on the blood of the One who spilled that blood for us? God created every one of us as a unique son or daughter, and breathed life into each of us with one goal, and that is for us to fellowship with Him through His Son. However, as soon as we are old enough to experience the temptations of the world, we turn our backs on Him, declare our independence from Him, request that He stay out of our lives, blame Him for everything that is wrong in the world, and worship His creations instead of The Creator. Yet, God still sent his own Son to be punished and die so that we can skip our punishment and stroll freely into Heaven, all of it having nothing to do with our works, and everything to do with His grace and forgiveness.

No matter how hard Jerry tried and what situation he would imagine in his attempts to justify, he could not honestly admit that he would ever give his own son or daughter's life in the place of someone he liked, let alone for a group of people who persecute him, spit at him, and deny his very existence. He continued to struggle with the idea over the next few days. He would intentionally watch people around him and take notice of their selfish interactions with others and their hateful actions towards one another for sometimes as meaningless as to gain one lousy position in a grocery line, or to state their dissatisfaction in the taste of their food. Millions upon millions of people roaming this earth with complete selfish motivations and no desire to even acknowledge their true Father unless they need a miracle to get them out of trouble. The more he watched, the more he wondered how God could see any value or reason to save us from our own self-destruction. With this question, Jerry's own self condemnation grew even heavier as did the desire to receive the wrath he felt he deserved grew even stronger.

The evening finally came that had been planned for Jerry and Patrick's first meeting. Jerry drove up to the coffee house and searched through the large glass windows to see if his sponsor had already arrived. Not being able to spot him, Jerry walked inside, stopped just as he passed the front door and scanned the room until he spotted a hand raised high in the air, and Patrick signaling to join him at his table. The reason Jerry had not spotted him was that he was looking at the tables against the walls or in the corners, where he assumed Patrick would want to sit for their private meeting. Instead, Patrick had sat right out in the open and could not be more centered among the customers than the table he had chosen. Jerry shook Patrick's hand and then took the chair across the table from his new sponsor. Patrick immediately reached into his briefcase, pulled out a paperback book and handed it to Jerry across the table. He read the title across the front cover, and it became obvious that it was a ledger, or diary, for the sole purpose of recording his progress through the twelve steps of recovery. He began flipping through the pages and scanning some of the bold chapter headings, when Patrick reached across the table and pulled the book out of his hands. As he shut the book and set it on the table in front of Jerry, Patrick began to tell Jerry his story. Now remember, this was after normal daily work hours, and in the dead center of a coffee shop that was packed full of college students and business people. Patrick's voice was as big as his stature, which was even more of a guarantee that additional tables were privy to the purpose of their visit.

After a few awkward minutes of prideful embarrassment, Jerry began to relax in his seat and realized that Patrick was not ashamed of his past whatsoever. As a matter of fact, he was proud of it and enjoyed sharing the story with whomever would listen. He was catching most of Patrick's story, but every once in a while, Jerry's mind would drift back to thinking about Patrick's pride and confidence that he exhibited so well. Here was a man telling him about the complete failure of his life, losing his kids, his job, and his freedom to a five-year felony drug sentence, yet he carried himself as if he had never lost anything. At that very moment, it hit Jerry. Patrick had indeed not lost. He was not a loser, but a winner, and he knew it about himself. Patrick could truly say that he had successfully conquered an enemy that kills most of the people that it attacks. He had also used that experience to intervene and save the lives of dozens of addicts since then, and had dedicated the rest of his life to save hundreds more. Jerry wanted that confidence, he hungered for that swagger, but realized it would take time and work to get there.

Once Patrick finished his story of slaying his personal Goliath, he sat back in his chair, crossed his legs, and pointed his hand towards Jerry with his palm up, as if to hand over the rest of the conversation to Jerry. Wishing now that he had not sat completely across the table from him and was a bit closer, Jerry's self-consciousness did not want to use the needed volume to talk over the other coffee drinkers. He started his story by telling Patrick about his background, his family, his career, and his demise. He admitted that he had lost all control and was doing whatever it took to get ahold of those pills when he couldn't get them from the doctor, including lying and sneaking them out of family medicine cabinets. He explained that throughout his struggles with the addiction, he had every desire to quit taking the pills, but he simply did not have the will power and strength to resist the temptations of easy opportunities. Jerry closed his story by accepting the fact that if this was the way in which God was going to use to help him quit, he has no room to argue because he sure could not do it on his own.

Patrick nodded his head, took a deep sigh and sat up from his relaxed position. He sat looking at Jerry's teary eyes as if to remember back when he was sitting right in Jerry's position; when it seemed all was hopeless and lost. Patrick finally broke his silence and explained that he had absolutely no doubt that Jerry would be successful in recovering from the addiction and living out the rest of his prosperous life. He grabbed the book that he had given Jerry, opened it up and signed his name on step number one. He then turned the pages, signed his name to step numbers two and three, and started to turn the next page when Jerry surprisingly asked him what he was doing? Patrick set the pen down in the crease of the book and explained to Jerry that in just the time it had taken him to tell his story, Jerry had successfully shown that he was passed steps one through three and was now ready to begin working on the fourth. Patrick turned back to the front of the book and began to paraphrase what he was reading in question form.

"Did you not just admit to me that you were powerless to the drug and that your life had become unmanageable?" Jerry nodded his head. "Did you not basically tell me that it was going to take a work of God to help you through this?" Jerry nodded in agreement again. "Did you not just honestly and completely open up and confess the wrongs you have done to people and yourself and haven't you made up your mind that God is the only one who can remove these shortcomings from your life and set you back on the right path?"

Jerry answered confidently that, indeed, that is what he has realized and understood of his current situation and prays that The Lord will get him through this. Patrick smiled at Jerry and exclaimed, "Then you are at the stage in your recovery where you will begin step number four." He clarified to Jerry that the steps must be taken seriously and must be accomplished before moving on. However, the first half of them are really a gauge of where the person is mentally, emotionally and spiritually. He went on to explain that everyone graduates through these first steps at their own rate, while some will never get past step number one, as they are the ones whose pride will never admit they are not in control. "As for you, Jerry," he stated, "You have fully accepted your part in this and what needs to be done in order to beat this demon. However, your problem is not that you don't want to accept responsibility. Your problem is that you won't let yourself off the hook and forgive yourself for this disease." As soon as Patrick said the words, Jerry's jaw muscles began to flex again, his teeth gritted with enough power to begin shattering his molars. Jerry flat-out hated himself and had no desire to be forgiven by anyone, and especially himself.

He did not have to say a word for Patrick to read exactly what was going through Jerry's mind. Jerry had no intention of earning any forgiveness. He was convinced that he did not deserve it and was solely motivated by his desire to take care of his wife and children, protect them from the evils of this world, guide them through their important life lessons, and provide them with everything they need to live and succeed. He owed them that, but owed himself nothing.

Patrick asked Jerry to leave the book closed and to not read step number four or begin making the list in the book until he had done one thing first. Jerry wrinkled his forehead in curiosity but agreed. Patrick instructed him to go home and read the book of Luke, and primarily chapter 15, verses 11 through 32, which is the story of the prodigal son. He asked that Jerry read the parable told by Jesus and then to meditate on it and look at the story from all the different perspectives. He told Jerry to ask himself how it would have felt to be the brother, the father, and finally the son. Then he instructed him to imagine if it were Jerry's son or daughter, would Jerry have done the same thing as the father in the story. If so, why? Patrick then instructed Jerry to call him in the morning and explain to him the conclusion he reached.

Confronting the Skeletons in the Closet

As he drove back to John's house that evening, Jerry thought back to the few times in his childhood that he had heard the preacher speak of the prodigal son. He recalled the story of a jealous brother and how the minister used it to explain how jealousy and envy can destroy us. He remembered another time when the preacher spoke of humbleness and the level of humility it took for the son to return to his father after what he did. Jerry was convinced that this was the reason Patrick had asked him to read the story, and that he was making sure Jerry was humble enough to return to his family after all of this was over.

After a quick dinner and a hot shower, Jerry crawled in his usual position on top of the blankets and propped his head up to read his assignment. As he covered the first few verses, the story's familiarity began to come back to Jerry. There was nothing new to him as he read how the son wanted his inheritance immediately instead of waiting for his father to pass away. It was the same story that he remembered as the son squandered and wasted all of the money, and when he was broke, all those who he thought were friends were nowhere to be found for help.

Jesus said, "A certain man had two sons. The younger son said to his father, 'Father, give me my share of the inheritance.' Then the father divided his estate between them. Soon afterward, the younger son gathered everything together and took a trip to a land far away. There, he wasted his wealth through extravagant living.

He continued to read further and realized that he had forgotten the part where the son had taken a job feeding pigs and resorted to begging to eat from the same trough as the hogs. At this point in the story, Jerry began to feel a slight resemblance to the son, as he wanted to return home but as nothing more than a slave, for that is all he felt he deserved to be.

When he had used up his resources, a severe food shortage arose in that country and he began to be in need. He hired himself out to one of the citizens of that country, who sent him into his fields to feed pigs. He longed to eat his fill from what the pigs ate, but no one gave him anything. When he came to his senses, he said, 'How many of my father's hired hands have more than enough food, but I'm starving to death! I will get up and go to my father, and say to him, "Father, I have sinned against heaven and against you. I no longer deserve to be called your son. Take me on as one of your hired hands."' So he got up and went to his father.

To this feeling, Jerry could completely relate and understood the satisfaction the son would have just to return to his home, even if it was not as a member of the family. However, Jerry could not understand the reaction of the father once he saw his son returning home.

While he was still a long way off, his father saw him and was moved with compassion. His father ran to him, hugged him, and kissed him. Then his son said, 'Father, I have sinned against heaven and against you. I no longer deserve to be called your son.' But the father said to his servants, 'Quickly, bring out the best robe and put it on him! Put a ring on his finger and sandals on his feet! Fetch the fattened calf and slaughter it. We *must celebrate with feasting because this son of mine was dead and has come back to life! He was lost and is found!' And they began to celebrate.*

He thought to himself, how could he forgive so easily and to the point that he sprinted down the road to meet his son and welcome him with the finest of robes, sandals and a feast? How could he not scold the son and at least punish him for a season, making him work as a slave to earn his way back into the home?

Jerry followed Patrick's directions and again read the story from the viewpoint of the brother. Again, he was in favor of some punishment but also thought that if it were one of his brothers, he would be happy to have him home.

Now his older son was in the field. Coming in from the field, he approached the house and heard music and dancing. He called one of the servants and asked what was going on. The servant replied, 'Your brother has arrived, and your father has slaughtered the fattened calf because he received his son back safe and sound.' Then the older son was furious and didn't want to enter in, but his father came out and begged him. He answered his father, 'Look, I've served you all these years, and I never disobeyed your instruction. Yet you've never given me as much as a young goat so I could celebrate with my friends. But when this son of yours returned, after gobbling up your estate on prostitutes, you slaughtered the fattened calf for him.' Then his father said, 'Son, you are always with me, and everything I have is yours. But we had to celebrate and be glad because this brother of yours was dead and is alive. He was lost and is found.'

Finally, Jerry read the story for the last time from the viewpoint of the father. He imagined Elaine or Allen as the prodigal child and started to think how worried he would be and how hurt he would feel. Jerry tried to think how the dad felt when he looked far down the road and on the farthest horizon could recognize the familiar posture and walk of his missing child. He agreed that there would be nothing but happiness and joy in his heart to see his Elaine or Allen return. He would know that the consequences they served that forced them to come home was enough and no more would be necessary.

Although Jerry was now extremely curious as to what exactly was involved in step number four, he had made a promise to Patrick to wait. A major part of his recovery agenda was rebuilding his integrity and character, and that meant in his own view of himself. Therefore, he fought the temptation to look in the book, turned off the lamp and began his nightly prayer to God asking for His protection of Maggie and the children, and thanking The Lord for the miracle provisions that He has provided to allow a roof to stay over his family's head and have food on their table. The story he had just read created an urge within him to "run back to his Father." Even though he knew he needed to continue his prayer and ask for forgiveness from God for his mistakes, Jerry could not bring himself to ask for something he did not feel he deserved. He simply finished the prayer in Jesus' name, and drifted off to sleep.

The early mornings were becoming a regular pattern to Jerry and by this time his eyes popped open well before his alarm would sound. After getting dressed and eating a couple pieces of toast, he climbed in his truck and began his morning drive to the treatment center. Arriving a few minutes early, he dialed Patrick's number on his cell phone and shared his thoughts and reactions to reading the story of the prodigal son. Patrick asked him a few more questions about the father's reaction and quizzed Jerry about how he would react if it were one of his children. Jerry admitted that he, too, would be welcoming and forgiving of his son or daughter in the same situation. Patrick paused for a few seconds and then instructed Jerry to understand that, in order to get through steps four through nine, he was going to have to believe that others have it in their hearts to forgive him. More importantly though, is the fact that God has already offered His complete forgiveness and all Jerry had to do is believe and accept the gift. Patrick went on to explain that just like the father of the prodigal son, his Heavenly Father is watching down the road for him and is waiting for Jerry to return home.

Immediately following dinner with John and his family, Jerry retreated to his room and opened the Twelve Step book to chapters four and five. It took only a few sentences for Jerry to understand what was being requested of him at this stage, so he took out a pen and a notebook and began to write.

> *"Step 4: We made a searching and fearless moral inventory of ourselves."*

> *"Step 5: We admitted to God, to ourselves, and to another human being the exact nature of our wrongs."*

As Jerry wrote his inventory list, and it began to overflow onto a second page, it became quite obvious that the absolute success of this step would be completely impossible without the guidance of The Holy Spirit. In the past, Jerry may have been able to humble himself to a point of admitting some wrongdoings and taking the necessary actions to correct his mistake. However, without the voice of the Holy Spirit in his life, Jerry always found a way to justify or excuse a majority of his shortcomings. Whether it was blaming others for forcing his hand or it was claiming pure ignorance, his pride was able to protect itself from having to accept full responsibility for all of his trespasses. With his pride humbled and shrunk to a minimum, Jerry was free to take an honest inventory of the garbage he had been stuffing and hiding for so long. As his list grew longer, he soon came to the full realization of the overwhelming number of skeletons that he continuously shoved in the closet and tried to ignore, justify and forget. He also realized that without completely cleaning out this closet, a full recovery would never be a possibility. If there were even one skeleton remaining, it would simply make it that much easier to begin adding bones to the closet again and resorting back to methods of self-medication for temporary relief. With a clean closet, however, our pride works in our favor, as we truly enjoy the freedom found in an empty and clean closet. We find a sense of arrogance in keeping it that way.

To be expected, Jerry's list was not completed in one sitting. Over the next several days, his conscience would occasionally dig up bones that he had buried in hopes to avoid the guilt and condemnation that they would bring every time they popped up out of the ground. This time, however, he was intentionally digging them up and bringing them all to one basket to deal with.

Several weeks had passed when Jerry finally exhausted all efforts searching the dark hiding spots of his heart and ran his pen out of ink. He was at last ready to sit down with Patrick and cross the bridge of Step 5. After some coffee and a little small talk, the discussion commenced and the crowded tables around them seemed to fade into nonexistence and no longer bothered him. The release and liberation experienced that evening had never before and has never since been matched. As the confessions poured out one by one, the weight of the guilt and condemnation rolled off his shoulders, ton by ton, causing an array of emotional releases from anger to sorrow and laughter to tears. With each short story he shared, Jerry's closet was becoming emptier and cleaner, and by the end of the long night, he left on an emotional high that no drug could ever match.

Jerry had every intention of following his typical nightly routine when he returned to John's house that night. Immediately following dinner and helping clear the table, he said his goodnights and headed for his room. He set his Bible at the head of the bed and placed his Twelve Step booklet next to it so he could begin investigating his next adventure. Sitting on the edge of the mattress, Jerry removed his shoes and then laid his head back on the bed next to his Bible in hopes of catching a second wind. When his head touched the mattress however, his mind had other plans. He awoke to his alarm ringing at its normal early morning hour and some slightly stiff back muscles caused by an eight-hour sleep with his legs hanging off the side of the bed. Steps four and five had taken Jerry beyond his emotional and spiritual borders and getting some good rest was just as important as mastering any one of twelve benchmark goals.

Removing the Skeletons from the Closet

Now that Jerry had uncovered all the hidden bones and experienced the most liberating act of confession, it was time for him to hand those bones over to God for final cremation. When leaving the coffee house that night, Patrick reminded Jerry of the sixth step and expressed the absolute necessity of knowing that the forgiveness of our sins is a promise that God cannot break, but is a gift of His mercy that can only be obtained through His Son, Jesus Christ.

But if we live in the light in the same way as he is in the light, we have fellowship with each other, and the blood of Jesus, his Son, cleanses us from every sin. If we claim, "We don't have any sin," we deceive ourselves and the truth is not in us. But if we confess our sins, he is faithful and just to forgive us our sins and cleanse us from everything we've done wrong.

1John 1: 7-9 (CEB)

It may be our upbringing and our early childhood vision of a judgmental and punishing god. Maybe it is the constant whispers of deception from the enemy. Possibly, it is from some other form of false information. Whatever the case, most of us, even Christians to some extent, hold an inaccurate perception of The Father and believe that there is a limit to just how much sin God will tolerate and forgive. Even though it is not written anywhere in His Word, we are often doubtful in His promises to forgive us as individuals. We feel that God has a scale on which he weighs our sins, and if the total is too high or if the weight of one sin is too large, we will fall from His grace and suffer His wrath with no hope for mercy. For Jerry, this is exactly where he stood just a few months prior. His lack of biblical wisdom was a huge contributing factor in his belief in a distant god who rewarded some of his more obedient children, harshly punished a few of those who he caught sinning, and pretty much ignored the rest of the world and left the outcome to pure chance.

When believing in a god such as this, there is not much hope in our salvation, let alone in any divine intervention to aid in our battle against the demon of addiction. If Jerry had reached the seventh step in his previous state of belief, as do many unfortunate individuals, his hopes in recovery and his confidence in the Twelve-Step Program would have crumbled and come to a disappointing halt. How can a person ask a vengeful god to forgive and remove shortcomings, and then have the faith that his god will grant his request? The fact is, you can't. However, Jerry's new understanding of who God truly is gave him the confidence to lay his shortcomings at the foot of The Cross and the faith to know that they would all be wiped clean and never again held against him.

Jerry was excited to reach out and share his revelation with Patrick. After a short phone conversation, the two agreed to meet for coffee again and prepare for Jerry's next bridge to cross. Once again, sitting in the middle of the afternoon coffee crowd, Jerry excitedly updated Patrick on the amazing breakthrough and the new life of freedom that he was enjoying. With his own experience and years of sponsoring dozens of other recovering addicts, Patrick had become well versed in identifying who was simply going through the motions to satisfy the requirements of the steps, and who was truly taking full advantage of the purpose of the entire process. Hearing Jerry's testimony was all he needed to know that Jerry did, indeed, take full advantage of the opportunity and was ready to move forward.

Patrick explained that before he set Jerry out to start his eighth and ninth steps, they needed to revisit the story of the prodigal son once again. Thinking that they had pretty much worn out that parable, Jerry was curious as to where Patrick was going to take it this time. He explained to Jerry that, just like the father, there are many people in this world who would drop everything they are doing to welcome him and celebrate his return to their lives. There are also a few, like the brother, who do not instantly act in forgiveness. They may take extra time to let go of a hurt his actions have caused, or they may never release the resentment towards his past behavior. Whatever the case, he encouraged Jerry to not become disheartened and to complete the steps with as much diligence and passion as he had throughout the first few.

He also read a verse from the book of Isaiah and explained to Jerry that if he is doing the Lord's will, he can be at rest in the Lord knowing that God will clear the way and soften hearts so His work can be accomplished.

I Myself will go before you, and I will level mountains. I will shatter bronze doors; I will cut through iron bars. I will give you hidden treasures of secret riches, so you will know that I am the Lord...

Not knowing exactly what was in store for him, Jerry agreed to trust Patrick's experience in the Lord's word, and in other's willingness to forgive. Before finishing his coffee and leaving the restaurant, he thanked Patrick for his time and promised he would call once he got started with the steps.

The next day of class was primarily dedicated to the graduation of one of the members. This was actually his second attempt at a recovery as he admitted he had failed the first time because he did not continue with step twelve, as the program required. For those who were unaware of step twelve, Mr. Corbett opened his book and read the description as well as a few examples of how some have dedicated their lives to the final step.

"Having had a spiritual awakening as the result of these steps, we tried to carry this message to addicts, and to practice these principles in all our affairs."

Mr. Corbett then asked each member to think about how he or she might plan to follow step twelve throughout the remainder of their lives. Some said they planned to earn their counselor's degree and begin working in the addiction recovery field. Others claimed that they would continue to attend meetings for the rest of their life and be a sponsor to as many addicts as they could. Jerry knew where he wanted to use his new knowledge, but also was sure that he would never be welcomed into a school again. So, he announced that maybe he would like to simply start a youth group for young addicts in his hometown and hoped to help some of the teens and their parents that struggle with addiction. He said he would have to wait and see if he would even be accepted back into his hometown before making plans to set up shop. Ironically, when Jerry retired to his bedroom that night and opened his book to the eighth and ninth steps, he realized that he was going to find out if his hometown would accept his return much sooner than he had expected. Just the thought of carrying out what was required of him awakened an anxiety inside of Jerry that was equal to sitting on the other side of the table from the prosecuting district attorney and his loyal sheriff.

> *"Step 8: Made a list of all persons we had harmed, and became willing to make amends to them all."*

> *"Step 9: Made direct amends to such people wherever possible, except when to do so would injure them or others."*

Tending to the Garden of Faith and Hope

In just the first couple of months, the seeds of hope were beginning to sprout and show signs of green life. Jerry was well over sixty days of being substance free, and had gained a better grasp on the actual events that took place at Christ's crucifixion. Because of it, he had started to understand that a personal relationship with his living God was not just a possibility, but it was also something for which our Father longs. To top it all off, Maggie had begun to send a few more frequent text messages and the two had started having a nightly phone conversation. They were short conversations and sometimes there was more silent time than talking, but the important thing was the fact that they were starting to talk.

In their last conversation, Maggie had asked if he planned to come home anytime soon. Jerry wanted nothing more than to be with her and the kids, and accepting it as an invitation, happily agreed that he needed to make a trip to mow the lawns and take care of some chores around the house. It could not have been better timing as well for Jerry, since steps eight and nine required him to be back home among everyone involved.

On his four-hour drive home, Jerry had plenty of time to begin thinking of those who he needed to add to his list. As the number grew, so did Jerry's anxiety. The more painful memories that he could dig up, the more people he realized he had harmed in one way or another. Whether it was a lie told directly to them, or a sneaky swiping of a couple pills from their cabinet that they probably never noticed, it did not matter. It was important for Jerry to clean out his garbage can conscience, and to do that, he had to add every one of them to the list.

Upon arriving in town on that Friday afternoon, Maggie was still at work. It would be another couple of hours before she would be home. Jerry took advantage of the time alone and built up the courage to stop by the house of a friend whose name was on his list. Jerry knocked on Rick's door and was immediately greeted by the barking of dogs inside the house. After a few seconds, the dogs quieted down and he could hear the unlocking of the handle. Rick opened the door and welcomed Jerry with a friendly, but slightly awkward hello.

Rick had been one of Jerry's best friends who had spent many of outdoor adventures with him, as well as working side by side with Jerry for several years. Rick was one of the first to notice the changes in Jerry's behavior and personality, and had caught on to Jerry's illness at its early onset. He had been a caring enough friend to confront Jerry with his concerns and desperately tried to convince him to request help. With his pride at risk and his profession at stake, Jerry denied any wrongdoing and admitted to taking only the pills he needed for his immense back pain. Even though Rick had not planned for the friendly intervention to go in the direction it did, by the time Jerry left, they were no longer on friendly terms.

Rick asked what he could do for him, and Jerry responded by requesting his company on the front porch chairs. The two men sat and started some small talk about how Rick was doing and the latest weather trends in the small town. Finally, Jerry built up the nerve and began making his first amends. "Rick, I came here to offer my sincere apologies and to ask for your forgiveness if you can eventually find it in your heart. You were the first person who had the courage to confront me with my addiction and showed that you cared, yet I lied to you and turned my back on my best friend." Rick slightly nodded his head as a small upward lift of the side of his cheek showed evidence of a faint smile. "I have no excuses and will not try to make any," Jerry continued, "but I am now well aware of how strong my addiction was and that it had become a priority over my friends, family and career. Now, it is going to take a lot of work and the rest of my life to earn those friendships back."

Now sitting with everything out on the table and his pride vulnerably unprotected, Jerry waited for any kind of response. Rick slowly turned and looked directly at Jerry. His half-hearted grin turned into a full smile and he began to speak. "Jerry, you will always be my dear friend and whether you came here today or not, I had already forgiven you. However, you will never know how much I appreciate you coming over and having this discussion with me. It means everything to me and also tells me I am getting my old friend back."

After a few more minutes of typical man small talk about the weather, their team's chances in the upcoming baseball playoffs, and the latest boasting of their children, Jerry stood up to leave and reached out for a hand shake. Rick grabbed his hand and pulled Jerry in for a friendly hug. He assured Jerry that everything would turn out fine and t he would be there for him if he ever needed anything. As Jerry climbed into the cab of his pickup and started the engine, he could not help but smile as he recalled what Patrick had last said to him. He knew that even though it was uncomfortable, it was not as difficult as he imagined. Patrick was correct when it came to God preparing the way and other's willingness to forgive.

Still having another hour before Maggie was due to be home, Jerry decided that he had it in him to make at least one or two more visits. He chose two more friends that he had drifted apart from during the whole ordeal, and still had time to stop by and visit with a cousin. All three stops yielded the same outcome as it did with Rick, and Jerry was beginning to understand why those steps were imperative. What first gave Jerry an anxiety attack to just think about, soon had become an addiction of its own. With each amends made, another chain would unwrap from his conscience and more weight lifted off his heart. He had never before felt so much relief and freedom from just one act of integrity, and did not want it to end until he had faced everyone he could. He finished that weekend visiting and calling almost every person on that list. He lacked a few individuals who he wanted to be sitting face to face with, and that included his parents. He also knew that the person on the very top of his list was going to be very last, and he was going to have to wait until the time and the heart was right. That person was Maggie, and Jerry could not treat her as someone on his list to check off. The hurt and disappointment of being married to a man who lived a completely separate life she knew nothing about was just too much to check off the list with one apologetic conversation. She was not ready for that step, and Jerry had to give her the space and time she needed until she was ready. Before that particular weekend, he was not sure if Maggie would ever be ready to have that conversation, but by the time Jerry was packing to leave on Sunday night, he felt a little more confident that one day she might. Maggie had opened up a little that weekend and asked Jerry a few inquisitive questions about the treatment center and the subject matter that he was learning. She inquired whether family was ever invited to attend, and asked him to bring home a book or two written on the topic of families and addiction. The most promising sign, however, was the fact that for the first time since that infamous April night, the two of them slept under the same blankets together and shared the center of the mattress instead of teetering on the farthest edges.

The four-hour drive back to John's house in the city again gave Jerry plenty of alone time to process all that had taken place that weekend. From discovering that the true nature of people are not at all different from the father of the prodigal son, to gaining a little more hope in his marriage, all in all the few days at home were a huge success. He knew he had a long way to go, and he may have only gained an inch on a hundred-mile journey, but at least it was an inch in the forward direction.

After arriving at John's house and visiting for a few minutes, Jerry went back to his room and unpacked his suitcase. Climbing back on top of the neatly made bed, he opened up the Bible and finished reading the book of Luke. Several of the parables made Jerry think and question if he truly was using and multiplying the gifts and blessings that God had given him. Taking an honest inventory of his heart, Jerry knew he had been falling very short in that category. Jerry had many God-given gifts and talents, and not one of those talents did he ever earn through his works. Intelligence, common sense, organization, leadership, communication and people skills are just some of the characteristics with which we either are born or will always lack. Knowing this fact, Jerry was well aware that he had not earned any of the blessings that had been bestowed on him and these blessings were also the sole reason of his success up to this point. However, he also could not remember the last time he had employed one of those gifts to glorify God or to help anyone besides himself.

Following the nightly routine that he had now made a habit, Jerry closed the Bible, turned off the lamp, and finished the day with a sincere conversation with the Lord. Jerry had always viewed prayer as a one-way phone call, where we thank God for what we have, ask him for forgiveness for the day's mistakes, and then close it out with a request for something we happen to need or want at the time. Once we are finished, we say the word "Amen", roll over and go to sleep, hoping that somehow our words will find their way through the clouds and cosmos and land upon God's ears. However, now Jerry was beginning to see things a little more clearly. God is not just some ultimate being that sits in a far off land with His angels keeping Him up to date with the latest world news and bringing millions of prayers in the form of telegrams. Jerry was beginning to realize the natural limits he had been putting on our supernatural Father. Just because we cannot fathom how something might be done, does not mean that God cannot do it. Science can try to explain how the first bit of matter came to exist or how the first living organism magically came to life, but they know it is simply unexplainable. They will tell you that if all of the conditions are right, then life can ensue. However, there is that one little, split-second, flash of missing information, and that is the very first instance where something went from non-living to alive. We cannot fathom it nor can we explain it, yet here we are, alive.

In the same manner, we may not be able to wrap our human minds around the fact; however, our God is indeed intimately involved in the details of every one of our lives. Each and every one of us were made with His desire to have a living relationship with Him and to rely on Him for all of our needs and wants. God is so involved in the details of our lives that He knows the number of hairs on our head at any given time, and like the father of the prodigal son, is just waiting for each one of us to come home.

Therefore, I say to you, don't worry about your life, what you'll eat or what you'll drink, or about your body, what you'll wear. Isn't life more than food and the body more than clothes? Look at the birds in the sky. They don't sow seed or harvest grain or gather crops into barns. Yet your heavenly Father feeds them. Aren't you worth much more than they are? Who among you by worrying can add a single moment to your life? And why do you worry about clothes? Notice how the lilies in the field grow. They don't wear themselves out with work, and they don't spin cloth. But I say to you that even Solomon in all of his splendor wasn't dressed like one of these. If God dresses grass in the field so beautifully, even though it's alive today and tomorrow it's thrown into the furnace, won't God do much more for you, you people of weak faith? Therefore, don't worry and say, 'What are we going to eat?' or 'What are we going to drink?' or 'What are we going to wear?' Gentiles long for all these things. Your heavenly Father knows that you need them. Instead, desire first and foremost God's kingdom and God's righteousness, and all these things will be given to you as well. Therefore, stop worrying about tomorrow, because tomorrow will worry about itself. Each day has enough trouble of its own.

Matthew 6: 25-34 (CEB)

With this new understanding of his Father, Jerry's prayers were becoming a little more than one-way requests. He was starting to pray to a God who is in the room with him in the form of The Holy Spirit. He sits at the foot of the bed, He rides in the passenger seat of the truck, and He places a gentle hand on our shoulder when whispering words of wisdom and guidance into our ear. The most important and impactful action required of Jerry was to do absolutely nothing. He had learned that the reason his prayers had always seemed to be a one-way conversation was that he did not know how to shut up and listen. Once Jerry started to learn to be still and allow God to speak, he also started recognizing the unlimited methods that God uses to communicate with us. Most of the time it is an overwhelming conviction in our heart, or a strong feeling that we know was not from our own making. Sometimes, it actually is a whisper in our conscience that tells us what we need to do or, and what it is from which we need to walk away. Other times His message is within His Word written in scripture. We often pick up the Bible to resume our daily reading, and the next thing we know, we have just received the answer to our most recent trial or difficulty that had been weighing heavily on our heart. The Lord sends friends, family or complete strangers with a message that they have no idea they just relayed, yet the message sends you directly to your knees knowing that it is greater than just some simple coincidence.

One such overwhelming conviction commenced tapping on Jerry's heart, and after a few days of ignoring it and dismissing it as nothing more than a suggestion from God, it became a strong tug, and finally turned into a suffocating squeeze that would not let him go another day without addressing it. On his first day back from his weekend break, Mr. Corbett announced that because the group had three members graduating in two weeks, he would like to encourage everyone to invite their spouse, significant other, and children. Now that Jerry had a couple of months under his belt, the shyness was long gone and he had become a brother within a special family of survivors. Once the invitation was extended, the rest of the group relentlessly attempted to persuade Jerry to bring the family. He gave several reasons why it would not work, including the four-hour drive, Maggie's job and her responsibilities at home. Not accepting any of his excuses, Mr. Corbett and the group, including a few newcomers, continued their daily peer pressure. God was speaking to Jerry through his classmates and the internal conviction had a death grip on his heart.

Not sure just how she would react, Jerry finally obeyed the Father's request and during their nightly short phone call, he asked Maggie if she, Elaine and Allen would come. By the silence from the other end of the line, it was obvious that it was not something that excited her very much. Maggie had never been a fan of crowds or even small group gatherings, and especially around people who she did not know. If Maggie had her way, she would prefer to live in a world no larger than her children and immediate family. Consequently, asking her to mingle among a group of strangers who share their most intimate feelings and expecting her to do the same would be like tossing a field mouse into a room full of hungry alley cats.

Maggie finally broke her silence by promising Jerry that she would think about it and might consider joining for a few minutes. He had been married to Maggie for almost twenty years and by this time, he had learned a lesson or two. One of which was the fact that the quickest way to get her to say no was to push her or try to rush her into a decision. Her willingness to at least consider the possibility was more than he expected, and he knew to leave well enough alone.

LANIER T. NORTHRUP

Sharing an Experience with the Apostle Paul

Over the next couple of weeks, the group discussed the summaries of a few in-depth professional studies of the brain and the effects of drugs and alcohol. What seemed to stick with Jerry more than any other factual conclusions was the fact that addictions are formed in the mid-brain. To most people, this fact is no more than trivia and may mean absolutely nothing. However, to an addict or the family of an addict, it helps to begin clearing up many questions and allows us to begin forgiving those who have hurt us.

Many friends and family members of addicts are often baffled and deeply hurt by the actions of the user. They have been lied to, stolen from, verbally rejected and abused, and even physically harmed by the addict during his or her quest for the next dosage. These actions are interpreted as direct and personal attacks, as well as a clear message that the addict has consciously chosen the substance over their love and relationship. Understandably, feelings are hurt, friendships are destroyed, and forgiveness is the furthest thing from their minds. However, once we learn the simple and basic functions of the brain, it becomes a little easier to understand how the addict was able to behave in that manner with complete disregard of others' feelings or wellbeing. In absolutely no way does it ever justify or try to excuse our actions, but it simply helps others comprehend what was actually happening in that head and may make it a little easier to forgive someday.

Jerry learned that the mid-brain's main function is for survival. One of the main functions of the frontal cortex is problem solving and reasoning. When we are faced with a life and death situation, the mid-brain turns on and takes control, as the frontal cortex takes a back seat. The cause being the simple fact that if we stand around and try to reason through a solution, we get eaten by the predator or hit by the oncoming car. The mid-brain simply tells the body exactly what to do in order to survive, which may be to hide, run away, or fight. Our survival brain simply says, "do", and we do. Unfortunately for some, it turns into the most embarrassing and humiliating moment of their life as the most effective method of survival chosen by their mid-brain at the time was to scream like a baby or hide themselves behind a woman and child. While others are a little more fortunate as their mid-brain decided that the best chance for survival was to attack the assailant and disarm them. This person is treated as a hero and given a statue on the front steps of city hall. Whatever the case, we truly cannot take any credit for our "heroic" or "cowardly" actions because most of us who are not trained in combat situations do not cognitively choose our actions in those situations.

The terrifying discovery is the fact that it is this mid-brain that becomes addicted to the dopamine effects of drugs and alcohol. What's terrifying about that? The simple fact that the brain associates the drug with survival, and just like the unpredictable actions of the person in a life or death situation, the addict's frontal cortex takes a back seat to the mid-brain when the next dosage is needed.

Not looking for justification or an excuse, however, this study did offer Jerry a little peace through understanding where many of his regretted actions came from. It also gave him a lifelong tool to fight off future temptations, obsessions and relapses. He was aware of situations that would trigger the mid-brain to begin firing up its motor, and was now excited to start learning the strategies to turn that motor off before it takes off.

In his room at John's house, like every night, he still refused himself the comfort of climbing under the blankets. As silly as that may sound to some, Jerry took it seriously and felt that some of life's simple luxuries were just too good for a man who had caused other people's lives to turn upside down. As for reading the Bible, it continued to be a nightly commitment for Jerry. It took reading and discovering a fact about the Apostle Paul of which he was unaware to convince him to let go of the silly blanket penance.

It had either been a detail that had never been shared in a church service that Jerry attended, a detail he daydreamed right through as a teenager or it was a detail intentionally set aside and preserved by God to expose to Jerry at the right time. Whatever the case, it was a detail that, once found, turned Jerry's entire outlook around. Jerry had always known how the Apostle Paul spent his life spreading the Gospel and the truth about who Jesus Christ is and what His death and resurrection accomplished for all people who would accept Him. Jerry knew the tragic end to the story and that Paul will always be respected as one of the great Christian martyrs. Embarrassingly, Jerry was completely unaware of Paul's life before he was a Christian.

By the time Jerry had finished the first four books of the New Testament, his knowledge and understanding of the Father's love, His sacrifice, and our lifelong mission, had grown from almost nonexistent to a daily desire to walk with the Lord. As he moved on to read the first few chapters of the book of Acts, the outcome was no different as Jerry's eyes were again opened to the scriptures in a new way. He was aware of the fact that after Christ's death, resurrection and ascension to Heaven, the apostles had performed many miracles of healing. However, it was the first time Jerry realized the message and importance of it all. This power of the Word was not bestowed on only the apostles and chosen individuals. It is indeed a power given to all who accept the Lord Jesus Christ through the power of The Holy Spirit. This includes me! Jerry thought to himself. We are all given the right and ability to have The Holy Spirit work through us as a vessel of power and healing. What is required of us is the willingness to give our lives to Christ and the faith to obey, even when we do not understand where His direction is taking us, or why.

Jerry was receiving blessings and knowledge from all sides. In the mornings, his recovery classes were teaching him the strategies to remain free of addiction for the rest of his life. In his nightly meetings and visits with his sponsor, Patrick, he was receiving the support that was more vitally important to his success than he had ever imagined. At night, just before dozing off to sleep, he was getting a full dose of God's word and a stronger relationship with the Lord. However, it was when he reached chapter nine of the book of Acts when his entire outlook of himself and his future took a turn towards true healing.

Meanwhile, Saul was still spewing out murderous threats against the Lord's disciples. He went to the high priest, seeking letters to the synagogues in Damascus. If he found persons who belonged to the Way, whether men or women, these letters would authorize him to take them as prisoners to Jerusalem. During the journey, as he approached Damascus, suddenly a light from heaven encircled him. He fell to the ground and heard a voice asking him, "Saul, Saul, why are you harassing me?"

Saul asked, "Who are you, Lord?"

"I am Jesus, whom you are harassing," came the reply. "Now get up and enter the city. You will be told what you must do."

Those traveling with him stood there speechless; they heard the voice but saw no one. After they picked Saul up from the ground, he opened his eyes but he couldn't see. So they led him by the hand into Damascus. For three days he was blind and neither ate nor drank anything.

Jerry was aware of the fact that Paul's name before becoming an apostle of the Lord was Saul. Yet, he was unaware that Saul's main ambition and aspiration was the persecution of Christian believers and preachers. Every morning, his motivation was to catch, imprison and even kill as many teachers of the Gospel as possible in order to stop the spreading of the Gospel.

When reading that the spirit of Jesus knocked Saul off his donkey, blinded him for three days and then set him out on a mission, Jerry caught himself asking why Saul was not punished more harshly and made to pay for his terrible sins. It set Jerry back against the headboard of the bed. He set the Bible down for the night and questioned his entire understanding of God, sin, punishment, and forgiveness.

Ananias went to the house. He placed his hands on Saul and said, "Brother Saul, the Lord sent me—Jesus, who appeared to you on the way as you were coming here. He sent me so that you could see again and be filled with the Holy Spirit." Instantly, flakes fell from Saul's eyes and he could see again. He got up and was baptized. After eating, he regained his strength.

He stayed with the disciples in Damascus for several days. Right away, he began to preach about Jesus in the synagogues. "He is God's Son," he declared.

Jerry pondered the very thought of this man committing such atrocities against the Father's people and then being instantly accepted by the Lord as a soldier of God who would become a hero to millions of Christians. Jerry then identified a slight similarity between his and Saul's story and it forced him to follow the word down a different, more selfish path. He thought to himself that here is a man whose sins were far more serious than those of his own were. However, when Saul faced his intervention, he suffered only three days of blindness and then was not only forgiven, but also then taken in by the Father, was used to spread the Gospel as the Apostle Paul, and to write numerous books of the Holy Bible. Jerry sat there in a manner of almost sulking in his current situation and asking how Saul could be so easily forgiven and yet he, for far less crimes, was suffering such consequences.

It took a few minutes but eventually, The Holy Spirit's voice began to break through Jerry's stubbornness and self-pity. Just as he finished mumbling the question under his breath concerning his perception of the injustice, Jerry's conscience was hit with a question that seemed to come straight from the Father. A question that asked Jerry to explain exactly how he feels he has been punished. Jerry sat for a while and then started to squirm on his bed as he could not list one example of God's punishment. In all actuality, God had never been punishing Jerry. As a matter of fact, God had been displaying overflowing mercy and grace to him. Jerry was the one punishing himself, refusing to forgive, and listening to the whispers of the enemy that were telling him that he had lost the Father's love and favor, and God would never use such a broken man.

The countless acts of God's grace that had been pouring out for Jerry suddenly became real to Jerry as he sat there on his bed that night. He started thinking about how he was taught in the university to classify student behavior; once is an incident, twice is a coincidence, but three times is a trend. He finally understood that indeed a trend had been taking place. A trend that displayed the undeniable intervention of a power greater than his own. Nothing that had been falling into place and turning in Jerry's favor could have ever been orchestrated by any person or by mere coincidence. It was undeniably the work of God and it had His fingerprints all over it.

That night was a major turning point for Jerry. He shared some commonalities with the Apostle Paul. They were both knocked off their high horse, their pride busted down to size, and then welcomed in to the family of God to begin doing His work. Just as District Attorney Thompson had said, the Lord did have plans for Jerry, but what those plans were was the mystery, yet a mystery that for the first time excited Jerry.

God Will Handle the Details...If You Will Let Him

Jerry's new life had quickly fallen into a patterned routine of the morning recovery class, afternoon work, late evening group meetings, nightly scripture reading, and late night sleep. Most of the time he couldn't tell you what day it was since he really had no reason to keep track. The date had quickly slipped up on Jerry, and Mr. Corbett reminded the class that the upcoming Friday was an opportunity for the families to join. He still had not heard a decision from Maggie and was hesitant to push her for an answer. However, he did need to remind her that the invitation was open and he would love for her to come. After getting off work that evening, he called Maggie and after some small talk about the weather and the kids, he asked if she had considered driving to the city for the family day. Again, she was hesitant to give her answer, but finally announced that Elaine and Allen did express their interest in attending, so she felt it was important to take them. She made sure to remind Jerry that she may only stay for a few minutes, but would let the kids stay for the day if they wanted. Jerry smiled and lifted his eyes to the heavens in acknowledgment of God's persuasive tactics and agreed with Maggie, telling her that he would be happy with however long she would decide to stay.

Late Thursday night, Maggie and the children arrived at her brother John's house, and Jerry welcomed them all in with big hugs and smiles. Even if nothing else was ever going to come out of this whole experience, one major result was for sure. Jerry saw his family under a light in which he had never viewed them before. Every minute with them should be treasured as a gift from God that can be taken at any minute. They were not just two mouths to feed who left clothes and dirty dishes wherever they walked. They were two, individual priceless possessions of God, who had been entrusted to Jerry during their time on earth. Jerry's main responsibility was to lead them to the Father through their faith in His Son, Jesus Christ. However up to this point, he had not done a very good job. If God were to hand out midterm grades, Jerry was sure he would be failing miserably. He knew he was being given the amazing and undeserved opportunity for a second chance at a whole list of failed obligations in his life. He was taking each one of them seriously, but none any more seriously than Elaine and Allen.

As anyone could probably imagine, Jerry did not get much sleep that night. With the recent peace that he had found in the Lord, he no longer had trouble getting a good night's rest. Nevertheless, the anticipation of tomorrow was a little too much for Jerry to simply sweep aside in his mind. He wanted the experience to have such an impact on Maggie that it would start a breakthrough in their relationship. Up to this point, they were living separate lives, and Jerry was experiencing all of the breakthroughs, blessings and victories. Maggie, on the other hand, was dealing with two teenaged kids, sports schedules, a twelve-hour workday at the school, laundry baskets, meals, and a husband in rehab. Anyone with even a little bit of empathy can imagine how Maggie might have been feeling.

Friday morning had arrived and after rushing around the house, speeding through traffic, and scrambling across the campus, the four of them walked into the classroom together and were immediately greeted by Mr. Corbett. Sensing the tension and nervousness in Maggie's eyes, he quickly broke the ice with a little humorous stab at Jerry, stating, "So this is the lovely family that has to put up with the pill popper." Mr. Corbett was a firm believer that if we cannot smile at our mistakes and honestly laugh at some of the stupid and silly things we did as addicts, then we will never be able to truly be set free. After he received a stunned look but also got Maggie to giggle a little, he then explained that it was okay because he was once a man who frequently woke up in his own fluids. The main thing is that it was all behind both of them now. Maggie's tense shoulders proceeded to fall as the anxiety and nervousness subsided, and her comfort level rose. Instead of visiting for just a few minutes, she appeared as if she might stick around until the mid-morning break.

Mr. Corbett started the day as he did every other day, with a prayer, a reading from the scriptures, and a brief embarrassing memory of his addiction days. He then honored the graduates of the day with an introduction and asked each of them to once again tell their story of what brought them to recovery and what they have discovered about themselves. Throughout the entirety of each person sharing their story, Maggie and the children's eyes seemed not to blink even one time. Having to pick their chins off the floor occasionally, they too began to realize that the disease does not play favorites and it is not prejudiced as to who it assaults. It will attack anyone and everyone, and absolutely no one is immune. By mid-morning, nobody in the room had a dry eye and it became evident that a little break was needed. Maggie and Jerry walked out onto the lawn and, for the first time, Maggie spoke of the elephant in the room. She said what had made her the most upset was wondering how he could throw away his career and be willing to throw away his family for something so meaningless. "I'm glad I came," Maggie said as she looked down at Jerry's shoes. "With just the three stories that I heard, I'm starting to see that it's not necessarily a conscious and purposeful decision to throw it all away. Since everyone in there has lost so much over their addiction, there must be something real about the disease."

About that time, Mr. Corbett approached Jerry and Maggie and asked if she wanted to participate in a couple's exercise. As Maggie always does when she is hesitant to volunteer for something she knows little or nothing about, she stood staring at him with one eyebrow lifted and awaiting more detail. He went on to explain that she and Jerry would sit facing each other in front of the group, and she would have the opportunity to tell Jerry exactly what his addiction has done to her and how his actions have hurt her. Looking directly at Jerry, Mr. Corbett passionately stated, "And your husband will say nothing except that he hears you and acknowledges your feelings." Maggie tilted her head, squinted her eyes, and gave a long, "Uhhhhh." He accepted her indecision and told her to think about it and if she felt like doing it after watching some other couples, Jerry and Maggie could take their turn.

Mr. Corbett returned to the room and slowly turned down the music volume, which still had everyone trained to return to their seats and get ready for the next activity. He called the first couple up to the front of the room where they sat in the chairs with their knees touching, hands on their own thighs, and looking directly at one another. There was an awkward silence which in most cases would have brought on some nervous laughter just to break the discomfort. This was different though. It was a silence that everyone respected, even the two teenagers sitting next to Maggie and their dad. The husband looked down at the ring on his left hand, began to spin it around his finger, and then started. "When this all came to a devastating reveal of what you were doing and who you had become, I had every intention of removing this ring from my finger and you from my life. I did not believe that I could ever find it in myself to forgive you." The broken man continued to walk her through every heart-breaking choice she had made and every shattering action she took throughout her addiction. With the outpouring of each bottled up injury, the emotional release became more and more visible. At first, what seemed to have to be forced out of his dungeon of painful memories, the charges were now freely flowing. With each one let out of its cage, the tension, anger and resentment was escaping with it. The groom of twenty years closed with a very blunt and candid declaration, "I was barely able to live through this once, and there is no way I could survive a second time. I know I vowed for better or for worse, but if you fall back into this hell again, I will not go with you."

The two sat looking into each other's eyes and then she bowed her head to collect her thoughts, lifted her eyes back to his, acknowledged what she had heard and agreed with his request. He reached across her knees and took hold of her hands, stood up with her and then pulled her into his arms. The group erupted into applause of congratulations as they walked back toward their seats. As the final handclap was fading, but before Mr. Corbett could utter the words that he had opened his mouth to say, Maggie stood up and announced with authority, "I'm ready to go!"

Assuming she meant the exercise had struck a sensitive nerve and caused the rise of some very hurtful emotions that she was not ready to deal with and was ready to exit the room, Mr. Corbett asked, "To go where?"

Maggie replied, "I need this and I need to do this while I still want to and before I talk myself out of it."

Completely stunned, Jerry stood up and followed her to the empty chairs in front of the room. This was not your typical Maggie. Even the children sat with their mouths wide open and lost for words. Maggie had always been the one who wanted absolutely no attention and wouldn't even get out on the dance floor unless it was dark, packed with people and she could disappear into the crowd. It took her almost two years to feel comfortable in front of a second grade classroom. However, to get her to say a word in front of her peers was worse than pulling a mule away from a bucket of sweet grains. It just was not going to happen.

Looking back at it now, Jerry owes the complete survival of his marriage to that very moment. The God-orchestrated moment where everything came together, where Elaine and Allen guilt her into going, where she heard something that persuaded her to stay past the break, and what she heard in her heart that convinced her to go against every fiber of who she was and step out on that limb. He knows very well that even if he had given her every opportunity to do this same exact exercise while alone in their home, she would have never taken the step. Even at the lowest point of his addiction, Jerry had never once raised a harmful hand to Maggie and she was never afraid of her husband, but she also would have never felt safe enough to confront him and her feelings the way she did that day. She might have eventually brought one or two of her painful memories to the surface to talk about, but the rest of all the wounds would have remained festering deep in her soul, as she would have continued to push them back down every time Jerry might do something that would bring back the memory. The continued suffocation of her genuine feelings and the true aching of her heart would have driven a wedge between them, not allowing them to ever grow any closer or heal any wounds. It would have only been a matter of time before Satan would have convinced them both to go their separate ways.

There was absolutely no doubt in Jerry's mind that God, the Father designed and carried out that entire day. There is no possible way that all of those pieces could have coincidently fallen into place. From Maggie even making the drive, to the chance that Mr. Corbett would have that activity scheduled was hard enough to believe. Yet, to add to it with Maggie going completely out of character and volunteering to be the second of only two groups to participate that day, was proof that God had His hands all over that room. As he recalled in amazement how everything worked together for that outcome, he could not help but to humbly smile at his doubts he used to have the first time he read Christ's words in the book of Matthew.

What do you think? If someone had one hundred sheep and one of them wandered off, wouldn't he leave the ninety-nine on the hillsides and go in search for the one that wandered off? If he finds it, I assure you that he is happier about having that one sheep than about the ninety-nine who didn't wander off. In the same way, my Father who is in heaven doesn't want to lose one of these little ones.

Until the last few weeks, Jerry had never really believed those words. He did not feel that he was worth God taking the time to look for and bring back to His flock. He always figured that if he slipped away, God was too busy solving the world's problems and planning the return of His Son to notice a single person had gotten lost, and He did not waste His time dealing at the individual level. That day had Jerry humbly eating his words as he realized that in order for the day's events to have fallen together as they did, God was involved in the details long before the sun rose that morning.

From that moment on, Maggie asked many more inquiring questions, freely shared her fears of the possibility of future disappointments, and showed a vested interest in Jerry's recovery. Granted, life was far from rainbows and clover-filled hillsides. Maggie had been thrust into the position of managing everything at home, while Jerry sat in his circle of new friends, sharing his most guarded secrets that not even she knew. The question frequently crossed her mind asking God why it seemed she was the one punished for Jerry's poor decisions. The good thing was that because of the day when Maggie let go of her inhibitions and let go of her bottled emotions instead of remaining silent, she had become more willing to share what she was feeling and free to express her dislike for her current circumstances, to put it nicely. Consequently, she was able to keep her frustrations and discontent from building up into a ticking time bomb with the children tiptoeing around her hoping they are not the one to set it off.

As Maggie and the kids drove off that evening and headed back home, Jerry fought back the tears of remorse. The tears were no longer for any self-pity he was feeling for himself or his situation. They were tears for the family who had been forced into their situation, and had never asked for it or done anything to deserve it. They were tears for a daughter who was spending her senior year in a damaged home. They were tears for a son who was at the age of needing his dad's guidance and wisdom, whether he acted as if he wanted or not.

They were tears for a wife who stood in a white dress nineteen years prior and looking into the man's eyes who she trusted to love her and keep her from all harm. Reality was soaking in, and Jerry was seeing the true effects of all his choices. Ever since he could remember, those three had taken a back seat to his career ambitions, when they should have been front and center of his attention. He had always expected the family to live according to his will and never paused for even a second to discover God's will. If he had, they surely would not have been in the situation they were now. It wasn't a secret that Jerry's will had failed him miserably up to this point. It was time to discover God's will for Jerry. Ironically, it was indeed time to begin steps ten and eleven.

"Step 10 – Continued to take personal inventory and when we were wrong promptly admitted it."

"Step 11 – Sought through prayer and meditation to improve our conscious contact with God as we understood Him, praying only for knowledge of His will for us and the power to carry that out."

Hiding Behind Jesus

Over the next few weeks, Jerry learned an unsurpassed amount of information concerning the human brain and how it is affected by addiction. Not only was the information important for Jerry in his own lifelong recovery, but it was imperative information when it comes to working with other addicts in the future. Anyone who is seriously considering following Step Twelve will need to fully understand and grasp the overwhelming stronghold addiction has on the brain and that there is only one combination that stands a chance of breaking that hold, and that is the combination of Christ and love.

Just as in Jerry's case, addicts are well known for sacrificing careers, money, cars, houses, and any other material possessions. Even though they are important, addiction will work its way up the hierarchy of personal value, and even become more essential than food, shelter and life in general. However, there is one "possession" that, when placed on the altar of sacrifice, the addict will consider giving up the addiction in order to keep, and that is the love of another human being. Whether it be a spouse, family member, friend, or child; the true love from and for that individual is at the top of the hierarchy, and very seldom surpassed by any addiction. It is the threat of losing those you love that will bring you to the point of surrender and a motivation for evicting the demon from your soul.

This realization could not have come at a better time for Jerry, as not only was his relationship with Maggie beginning to heal, but the Lord was also handing out blessings of grace by the handful. About half way through the recovery program, another relative of Jerry asked him if he would be interested in a job operating heavy equipment. Arthur explained that the job would provide a bit more money than he was making at the time. Loyal to John, Jerry struggled with the decision. He knew it was an opportunity to begin providing the family with the financial support that he once was. He also felt that he owed John, as he and his wife were the first to reach out when they really did not have to. Jerry also knew that any large construction company follows a specific hiring procedure, which includes a detailed background investigation. Even though the state was committed to dropping all charges, at this point they still remained current and would be there for another several months. With this hanging over his shoulders, Jerry arrived at the conclusion that it was best to stay right where he was.

However, apparently that was not where God wanted him. A couple of weeks had passed, and Jerry received another call from Arthur asking him to reconsider. Jerry explained to him that he did not believe he would make it past the background check and it would be a waste of time to fill out the application. Later that afternoon, Jerry received another phone call, but this time the voice on the other side of the line was unfamiliar. He introduced himself as Mr. Copeland, the vice president of the construction company. He explained that he typically did not involve himself with the hiring of field crew. However, when Arthur had mentioned wanting to employ Jerry regardless of his legal status, something weighed heavily on his heart and he felt he needed to reach out to Jerry. He asked Jerry if he wouldn't mind sharing his construction experience, and explain his current legal situation. Jerry did exactly that, as he told him of the many building projects he had completed, the equipment he had operated, and then moved on to his current situation. Feeling that it was irrelevant to the job, Jerry never did tell Mr. Copeland of the career that he was in when becoming unemployed. He simply shared the truth that over years of spinal surgeries, he had become dependent upon painkillers to the point that he lost his job and was facing legal consequences. He went on to explain he was fully dedicated to the recovery program and shared the fact that, in a few months, the state was committed to dropping all charges if he was committed to recovery.

After answering all of Mr. Copeland's questions, Jerry was surprised but also quite torn to receive a healthy offer to go to work for the nationwide construction firm. He explained to Mr. Copeland that he would talk it over with Maggie and give him an answer in the coming week. After hanging up, Jerry sat in his pickup truck amazed that a person of Mr. Copeland's stature would even bother with something that he employed others to handle. This was during an economic time when most of the construction labor force was unemployed and there were thousands who were more qualified than Jerry and applying at such firms by the hundreds. Watching the Lord's hand at work, once again it became obvious to Jerry that this was the path that God wanted him to follow. It was not going to be easy to tell John of his plans. He was not sure how Maggie might react, but Jerry had understood that Step 11, "praying only for knowledge of His will for us and the power to carry that out" was not going to be easy.

Even though Jerry was convinced that John would be disappointed in his decision to leave, the outcome was far from what was expected. John and his wife knew that this was temporary and they also knew that Jerry had a family for which to provide. Contrary to Jerry's expectations, John and his wife were excited about the opportunity and encouraged Jerry to take the job before it was too late. Maggie, on the other hand, was not so sure. She, indeed, knew that the family needed the income to pay the bills and keep food on the table. However, she had already spent several months filling the shoes of both at home, and the thought of continuing while Jerry worked on the road was not too thrilling.

It was not the most practical or ideal situation and living arrangements, because it required Jerry to travel and reside in motel rooms, while Maggie stayed at home and continued her role as mother and father. However, it did provide income that matched his former principal's salary and would reestablish financial security for his family. After several conversations with Maggie and numerous trips to his knees, Jerry finally did accept the offer as another door of grace and mercy that God was asking him to walk through. Maggie and Jerry were not fond of the idea of Jerry returning home for no more than a weekend per month, but at the time and under the current circumstances, it was the only sensible choice. They knew it would be difficult, but resolved if they were able to pull through the last few months of trials, they were confident they could make it through this challenge for a while as well.

Once cleared with the district attorney, Jerry began work with Arthur in the afternoons and set out on his last few weeks of his recovery classes. All seemed to be going great and headed in a direction that Jerry would never had imagined just a few months before. Allen was excelling in his junior high years in his academics as well as athletics. Elaine graduated from high school and was on her way to continuing her education and softball career at the collegiate level. Maggie was beginning to get back into the daily routines of her teaching career and enjoying the days that were no longer filled with a bombardment of questions about she and Jerry. Enjoying such a blessing from above, Jerry often questioned how a person would even consider relapsing into the addiction after going through such difficulty and coming out the other side with such success. As Jerry would tell anyone today, be careful what you ask for because the answer to your question will soon be knocking at your door.

The final few weeks of treatment came and went in a blink of an eye. Jerry proudly received his recovery coin on graduation day and was informed of one shortfall that he still needed to accomplish before his recovery could be complete and firmly planted in Step 12 for the remainder of his life.

> *Step 12: Having had a spiritual awakening as a result of these steps, we tried to carry this message to addicts, and to practice these principles in all our affairs.*

Mr. Corbett explained to Jerry that in order to successfully live in this step, he had to find it in his heart to forgive himself and let go of the guilt. As expected, Jerry's reaction began with the clinching of his teeth, evident through the bulging of the cheek muscles that tensed up at the very thought of self-forgiveness. He continued to hold on to the belief that if he even thought of forgiving himself, he would be excusing and justifying his actions, for which there was no justification. After a long pause of silence, Jerry revealed exactly how he felt about the matter. "I'll tell you what, Mr. Corbett. The day that I can find someone who is better off because of the mistakes I made, that will be the day that I consider even starting to forgive myself. Because all I know of are those who were hurt and suffered because of my mistakes, and for that, there is no forgiveness." Knowing that it was something he would have to live with through eternity, or at least until he was lowered into his final resting place, he smiled at Mr. Corbett and agreed, "But I'll work on it."

Just as Jerry completed treatment classes, his daughter Elaine was starting her first semester of college. His current construction project was scheduled to keep him in the city for a few more months, and with Elaine moving to the city as well, the two decided to save a little money and share an apartment. Now, rightly so, some of you are probably thinking that this was definitely not the way a college freshman would prefer to spend her first year away from home. However, the details orchestrated by our heavenly Father are never ending, if we just allow Him to do His work.

Ever since that infamous day that changed everyone's life, Jerry and Elaine had simply lived as acquaintances who shared the same last name. There was absolutely no discontent or loss of love between the two, but they both seemed to drift into their own worlds and agendas. Of all the people on the earth, Elaine was the last person Jerry ever wanted to disappoint. He was the leader of the house, the knower and doer of all things, and the rock his little girl stood on. Seeing the effects that turn of events had on his daughter, Jerry seemed to let go of the hopes of one day standing on that pedestal for Elaine again. After just a few short weeks with the two of them under the same roof, their father-daughter bond reignited and began to grow even stronger than before. Elaine's need for assistance with college courses was gladly met by her dad's eagerness to spend quality time together. Jerry's need for dinners that were healthier than a microwave burrito, and for the companionship that had been missing for months, were both gladly met by Elaine's eagerness to rebuild their fading relationship. What seemed like an apparent inconvenience to a first-year college bachelorette, turned out to be another incredible blessing with God's special touch of care and love, In hindsight, it came with perfect timing again. Looking back at it now, it was the only opportunity and time that would have ever been available for the two to mend their bonds, because Jerry was unknowingly headed for several destinations around the country, while Elaine would soon be headed for the farthest side of the country to continue her softball career.

After completing the local construction project, Jerry's company was preparing to move on to the next assignment, and Jerry was expected to follow. The only problem was it was three states away and no longer a four-hour drive on a Friday evening to visit his family. Again, Maggie and Jerry discussed their current situation and reluctantly agreed that he should follow the work and pray for the day that a job will be available for him to be back at home. So, Jerry packed his suitcases, said a tearful goodbye to Elaine, and began his long drive to the motel room that would be his home for the next year. Jerry drove away from home that day thinking the most difficult aspect would be the numerous weeks apart from his family. He and Maggie were beginning to have breakthroughs and enjoying whatever time they had together. He and Elaine were closer than ever before, and Allen was beginning his high school years and needing the influence of his dad at home. Jerry knew that leaving his family at this stage for weeks at a time was going to be one of the hardest things to endure. However, he had no idea he would also be engaging in the toughest spiritual battle he would ever face, and it would answer his question he had concerning the addicts who fall to the temptation of a relapse.

Knowing that his addiction was not limited to only opiate pain pills, and that it would easily transfer to another element, Jerry was committed to an abstinence from all mind-altering substances. This meant even though he had never battled with alcohol, he knew very well his brain would quickly latch onto the available bubbling brew and easily substitute it for the vacancy left from the absence of the narcotics. Knowing that he used to enjoy an occasional nightcap or a couple of drinks with a friend, this too would no longer be a part of his life. The problem, however, was the fact that drinking was a huge part of everyone else's life.

Upon arriving at the hotel parking lot, Jerry noticed his fellow construction crew members congregated around a barbeque grill. He transferred his luggage and belongings into his new room and then answered the invitation to join the group. As he stepped into the circle of coworkers and towards the grilling meats, an outstretched hand that was holding an unopened bottle of beer greeted him. With dozens of eyes on him and smiles welcoming him to their evening routine, the peer pressure was greater than he had ever remembered in high school. Thinking quickly, Jerry thought up an excuse and blamed his upset stomach on his unwillingness to accept the gift. Instead, he grabbed a soda from the ice chest and sat down to eat with his new friends.

Each evening after work, the offerings would continue, and Jerry would again express his gratitude but turn down the alcoholic beverage. He assumed that with time, the group would come to realize that he was not going to drink the beer ,they would stop offering and simply quit trying. However, his plan did not play out so smoothly. After a couple of weeks, the donation efforts did not stop. As a matter of fact, they came even harder and more persistent. Jerry faced questions about why he would not have a drink with his friends. Some persisted that one drink would not kill him. Others jokingly probed into his religion and asked if he was an elder in the Salt Lake City temple.

It was not long before Jerry started hearing the whispers from Satan and his demons, who repeated the same questions. He soon began to ask himself what one innocent drink would hurt. He started to reason that his problem was never with alcohol, so why did he have to give that up as well. Not only had Jerry stopped going to any recovery meetings, he was also drifting away from his daily dose of the word and his daily conversations with his Heavenly Father. Consequently, his ears and heart were beginning to tune out of God's frequency and tuning into the messages from the enemy. The problem is that no matter how tough we want to imagine ourselves or what Hollywood movies we have watched in the past, we are no match for Lucifer and his minions. Without the full armor of God, we are easy prey, and Satan loves nothing more than an ignorant human being who believes they can stand up to his powers alone and unprotected.

> *Finally, be strengthened by the Lord and his powerful strength. Put on God's armor so that you can make a stand against the tricks of the devil. We aren't fighting against human enemies but against rulers, authorities, forces of cosmic darkness, and spiritual powers of evil in the heavens. Therefore, pick up the full armor of God so that you can stand your ground on the evil day and after you have done everything possible to still stand. So stand with the belt of truth around your waist, justice as your breastplate, and put shoes on your feet so that you are ready to spread the good news of peace. Above all, carry the shield of faith so that you can extinguish the flaming arrows of the evil one. Take the helmet of salvation and the sword of the Spirit, which is God's word.*
>
> Ephesians 6: 10-17 (CEB)

Jerry continued to fight the good fight, staying clean and sober one day at a time. He did finally tell a few of his closer coworkers that he had once had a problem with addiction, and because of that had chosen to give up drinking alcohol. Ironically, and in hindsight, Jerry wishes he had done so much earlier since his friends were very accepting of his excuse and supported him by always having a few sodas handy during their evening gathering times. Jerry felt proud of his strong stance and was building up his confidence in a life of sobriety.

However, Satan was just getting started, and he was saving his heavy artillery for future attacks that would come at the right moment of weakness.

A few months had passed, and Jerry was working six and seven days a week, sending very hearty paychecks to the family checking account. His long days and short weekends became a blur and Sunday church services and evening Narcotics Anonymous meetings were no longer a part of his schedule. His focus was no longer on his recovery, but on his career and getting back to being the provider for the family and the man upon who they all depended. Just as any great general would do in the midst of a war, Satan waited patiently for Jerry's alertness to fade and his attention to be focused elsewhere, and then he attacked.

After a few weeks of blistering cold and snowy winter days in the Midwest plains, the conditions can drive even the healthiest man to a point of frustration. For Jerry, however, the weather took a toll on him and he was failing to hide it from his coworkers. Every cold morning, the eight-inch titanium plates, rods and screws that held Jerry's spine together were letting their presence be known, making the simple tasks of climbing into his dump truck or bending over to tie his bootlaces a monumental task. Jerry kept aspirin handy and made sure to do some warm up stretches each morning in attempts to avoid a major back injury, with which he was much too familiar. He knew that he needed only to get through the winter season to be fine, and that was just a short couple of months away. He made up his mind to grin and bear the discomfort and to push through until the springtime sun thawed the ground. However, the enemy had other plans in mind, and set some vicious traps for Jerry.

During one of the mornings, Jerry finished his morning report, left the field office and started walking toward his piece of equipment. A coworker of Jerry called him over the radio and asked Jerry if he would bring a pair of gloves he had forgotten to take from his personal truck. He explained to Jerry that the gloves were buried deep in the console between his front seats and told him that if he dug below the papers, old sunglasses, and used coffee cups, he would find what he was looking for. Jerry agreed and took the detour over to the man's truck. While cautiously digging to the bottom of the compartment, Jerry heard a familiar rattling sound that called for him like a long lost lover and for the moment, was sweet music to his ears. Digging a little deeper, Jerry came up with exactly what he had imagined he heard and the low-hanging fruit was perfect for the picking. It was a bottle of year-old painkillers, and was full to the top. Jerry's heart began to beat, his hands shaking, and his breaths becoming rapid and short. He began to imagine the relief he could have if he just took one of them. Then he envisioned the pleasures and daily comfort if he was to pocket the whole bottle. There is no way he would even miss these things. They're a year old, and he probably doesn't even know they are in here. Plus, even if he did miss them, it's obvious he hasn't used them in such a long time, he wouldn't even realize when they had disappeared.

It was too easy and much too convenient to pass up. After locating the gloves and stuffing them in his jacket, Jerry opened the cap to the pills and began to pour a few out into his left palm. While counting out the doses and figuring out the number of days of euphoria he could shove in his pocket, like a flash of lightning, a series of visions struck Jerry deep in his soul as if to transport him physically back in time and placing him in the exact moment and raw emotions. First, Jerry was pulled back into the body of his slumped-over self, sitting at the kitchen table while Maggie stood behind him desperately wishing she could wake up from the nightmare. Then, he was sitting on the couch staring into the eyes of his disbelieving children as their entire superhero image of their father disintegrated before their eyes. Just before the memory of reaching out to hug his children, he was pulled to the courtroom table where he sat across from the district attorney and feeling the overwhelming fear and being at the complete mercy, and his freedom under the absolute power of another person's choice. Finally, Jerry's conscience was thrown into the position of standing in front of Patrick as he explained his true purpose for being at the Narcotics Anonymous meeting and searching for a sponsor.

Jerry's radio sounded off again and shook him out of the daze. "Did you find my gloves?" his friend asked. Jerry poured the pills back into the bottle, screwed the lid back on tight and tossed it to the bottom of the compartment. He grabbed his radio, answered that he was on his way with the gloves and would be there shortly.

Throughout the remainder of the day, it seemed as if the truck called out to Jerry every time he passed by in his piece of equipment. From a simple temptation that started out that morning, by midafternoon it had become a complete obsession. As quitting time approached, a sense of panic began to take over and the anxiety was twisting his stomach into knots. The voice continuously reminded Jerry that if he did not grab the bottle soon, it would be gone and he would probably not get another chance like it again. He began to think up an excuse for returning to the pickup truck, such as leaving his keys on the man's front seat, or dropping some money out of his pocket when he was grabbing the gloves that morning. Every time Jerry would lift the radio to his mouth and begin to press the button to give his excuse for stopping by the parked truck, another flash from the past would consume his thoughts, forcing him to drive his dump truck passed the parking lot and continue on his route.

There was a spiritual battle taking place in the cab of the dump truck that day. This was nothing imagined and was as real as you sitting there reading these words. The battle that was being fought over Jerry that day and the protection wrapped around him is only possible for those who place their trust in the one true God.

As our third step tells us, "we are to make a decision to turn our will and our lives over to the care of God as we understand Him." However, when relying on a god that we choose to invent and understand in our own minds, we might as well be relying on only ourselves to fight the ferocious battles against a much more powerful enemy. God is not who we decide to make Him. He is exactly who He says He is and if we choose to believe in something or someone else, good luck having that imaginary friend fight an impossible battle for you.

You may be sitting there right now in total disagreement and stating that you choose not to believe in the God of the Bible because you can't see how a loving God would allow such atrocities and devastation to take place on the earth. The fact is that they are only atrocities and tragedies to those who are not believers and who do not understand the concept of eternity in heaven. For those who do not believe in, nor comprehend the meaning of eternity with God and our loved ones, that statement is extremely offensive and seemingly heartless as well. For those who do understand eternity, do grasp the fact that our life is but a blink of an eye and what we think is so atrocious here on earth, is nothing but a stubbing of a toe once we leave this place and are sitting at home with our Father and loved ones for the remainder of eternity.

I believe that the present suffering is nothing compared to the coming glory that is going to be revealed to us. The whole creation waits breathless with anticipation for the revelation of God's sons and daughters. Creation was subjected to frustration, not by its own choice—it was the choice of the one who subjected it—but in the hope that the creation itself will be set free from slavery to decay and brought into the glorious freedom of God's children.
Romans 8: 18-21 (CEB)

On the other hand, for those who choose to believe in a non-existent god because they want to rebel against the Creator for allowing them to feel such pain as the loss of a loved one, you have a terrible revelation coming your way. Because of your refusal and denial of the one true God and His Son, your rebellion will lead you straight to the one eternal place that is so immensely painful, that the loss of a loved one here on earth will feel nothing more that the stubbing of a toe. You now are probably asking why we would worship such a God who would send us to a place like hell. That is another misunderstanding, about which you really need to sit down and discuss with your pastor so you are hearing the truth instead of the voice from the enemy. In general, God does not send anyone to hell except for Satan. It is simply our choice of whom we will follow. If we choose to follow Jesus Christ, then He will lead us to the Father in Heaven. Alternatively, if we choose to follow the lies of Satan, we will follow him straight to where God has planned for him, and that is the eternal fires of hell. Our loving Father has no desire to lose any of us to the enemy, but He also gave us free will, and it breaks His heart to watch us use that free will to walk ourselves right down the path of destruction.

Go in through the narrow gate. The gate that leads to destruction is broad and the road wide, so many people enter through it. But the gate that leads to life is narrow and the road difficult, so few people find it.

"Watch out for false prophets. They come to you dressed like sheep, but inside they are vicious wolves. You will know them by their fruit. Do people get bunches of grapes from thorny weeds, or do they get figs from thistles? In the same way, every good tree produces good fruit, and every rotten tree produces bad fruit. A good tree can't produce bad fruit. And a rotten tree can't produce good fruit. Every tree that doesn't produce good fruit is chopped down and thrown into the fire. Therefore, you will know them by their fruit.
Matthew 7: 13-20 (CEB)

That evening after work, Jerry chose not to join the crew at the nightly parking lot cookout. Instead, he retreated to his room and took out his binder of notes from class. He opened up to the section that was labeled "Relapse Prevention" and began to refresh his memory. As he flipped through the pages, he found one repeating idea he had highlighted, underlined and written numerous times as a note to himself. It was the fact that there might be several methods to attempt when faced with the threat of relapse, but the most effective is to get down on his knees and hide behind Jesus Christ. We are not strong enough nor equipped to go face-to-face and toe-to-toe with Satan or his demons. Without the Armor of God and The Holy Spirit standing in front of us, our self-help religion is worthless, weak and an easy defeat. It is imperative that we have the one true God in our corner, because our imaginary god is not going to show up for the fight.

Jerry read on in his notes and found several places where he had listed some techniques for overcoming temptations. As he read his handwriting, he could recall Mr. Corbett's voice as he shared examples of how each one had saved him from a disastrous relapse. On several occasions, Mr. Corbett called his sponsor and shared his struggles. Other times he called or talked to a loved one and simply told on himself. He explained that by being honest and confessing our misguided thoughts, we will be amazed at how quickly the cravings will subside. Nevertheless, Mr. Corbett could not stress enough the importance of going straight to our knees and straight to the Lord for help. It is through our prayers and constant reading of God's word that we can and will stay clean one day at a time and for the rest of our lives.

Jerry knew very well he had drifted away from the fellowship of other recovering addicts, but most importantly the fellowship with other Christians and with God. If he did not find a way to get back into a regular routine of meetings, church, scripture reading, and prayer, he was eventually going to lose a battle and, ultimately, the war. Then, Satan would be standing victoriously over Jerry's house with another destroyed family as his trophy.

No temptation has seized you that isn't common for people. But God is faithful. He won't allow you to be tempted beyond your abilities. Instead, with the temptation, God will also supply a way out so that you will be able to endure it.

1 Corinthians 10: 13 (CEB)

After a short search in the local telephone directory, Jerry was able to locate a church. He desperately tried to sneak in and out of the first couple of Sunday services, but the regular attendees were not going to allow it. While trying to walk out unnoticed, a few members stopped him and welcomed Jerry to the family. It seemed that the people were genuine and sincere. He felt comfortable among the small congregation, and most importantly, the teachings were fully Bible based. Becoming more relaxed amid his new friends, and with a little bit of asking around, he was also able to find a couple of addiction groups that met twice a week in the little Midwestern town. The support from fellow recovering sufferers and the fellowship with other believers had a definite and instant influence on Jerry's thoughts and obsessions with the bottle that laid in the console and was just waiting to be taken. Within just a matter of a few weeks, the winter days were giving into the spring weather. He was right back in shape and out of pain, and the bottle of pills were out of mind. Most importantly, Jerry was filling his nights with God's word and some important discussions with God about his family situation. Don't think for one minute that the Lord was not listening.

The Gift of Redemption

By springtime, Jerry's transformation was beginning to take full shape and he was viewing the world through a different set of eyes. He had hoped that someday he could return to his normal life, but was now realizing he wanted very little to do with the old "normal." Just as the court's attorneys had promised, on the anniversary of the indictment date, they forgave all charges and wiped his record clean. With the added weight taken off their shoulders and the allowance of more sunlight to shine on their life, whenever he was able to spend a few days at home, Jerry and Maggie were free to redirect their focus onto each other and their children. He saw glimpses of hopefulness in his marriage, and Maggie began to find room in her heart to feel hope as well. Before they knew what was happening, they were growing closer, and subtle signs of love were beginning to resurface. It was not the same love that had brought them to their wedding vows though, but a love between a man, a wife and God, who had endured a firestorm together that nobody could ever imagine unless they, too, had walked through it and survived. It was a love that withstood the fires of pure hell and was the epitome of the vows of "for better or worse." Jerry's pride had been put in check over the last year, and he fully realized that the blessings he was experiencing were nothing less than an expression of God's grace and love for His children, which was also far from over for the both of them.

Even though Jerry was enjoying the abundance of blessings that he had never expected to unfold, he was just like the typical person who tends to focus on what they do not have instead of the amazing gifts that we do have. He was extremely happy with the closeness that he and Maggie were beginning to feel again, but it also brought on a tremendous feeling of emptiness. Jerry was now starting his second year away from his family and trying desperately to figure out how he could either get home or find a career where they could have a home, instead of living in a random hotel.

The irony of the whole thing is just how the Lord works and prepares us for what He has in store. We never seem to realize what God is doing in the present and typically complain and belly ache about why we are in the current situation. It's not until we find ourselves standing in a miraculous place of blessing when we realize that it would have never been possible without walking through the rough times.

God knew very well that Maggie and Jerry were not ready to be under the same roof just quite yet. They needed to see the value in each other and understand the true meaning of loneliness before they could fully appreciate each other's company and love.

There is no statement truer than the words of an anonymous poet who wrote, "Absence makes the heart grow fonder." Through the first year of his new job on the road, Maggie and Jerry had become fully aware of their genuine and unconditional love for each other. If there had ever been a shred of doubt that the two would stay together, that doubt had been erased just like Jerry's legal record. They felt nineteen again, and when together, they could not be separated for more than a second. Walking hand-in-hand, sitting cheek-to-cheek and cherishing every moment together, they dreaded the hour that would take Jerry back on the road for another four to six weeks. Each goodbye became more difficult to say, and they began to question just how much longer they could stand the lifestyle. What they were not aware of was God's behind-the-scenes orchestration, which He tends to keep secret from us until His works are revealed in complete wonder and amazement.

During the closing week of the current construction project, Jerry was called to the regional office to meet with the vice president. The call brought back memories of a similar curiosity and anxiety of sitting across the table from the district attorney and his lawman. He couldn't help but wonder if it would be news of being transferred to a project even further from home, or perhaps even worse news that his services were no longer needed. However, when he met with Vice President Copeland, he found it was neither one of his worrisome assumptions. In fact, what it was, once again left him standing dumbfounded, staring into the distance in complete amazement, and praising God for the blessings that he never earned and absolutely did not deserve.

Apparently, more than six months after being hired, Jerry's professional resumé had resurfaced on the desktop of the company vice president. Why the secretary had not filed it with the rest of the employee paperwork months ago, no one can say for sure. Jerry had his suspicions, and God was on the top of the suspect list. Just as strange, was what persuaded Mr. Copeland to thumb through a year-old job application of a field hand? Whatever was the case, Mr. Copeland noticed for the first time that Jerry held a master's degree and questioned himself about where Jerry might prove more valuable to the company: running machinery; or running entire projects? With that in mind, the management team began to closely evaluate Jerry's field work and after a few weeks, determined they would offer him the promotion. Just like that, Jerry was digging through his closet for his dress shirts, blowing the dust off his neckties and hanging his family pictures on the walls of another office. Unfortunately, the office was located two states away from Maggie, but the management position offered some extra flexibility in his schedule and would frequently allow more rendezvous with Maggie and the kids. It also gave them a location where they could eventually call home and live out the rest of their lives together.

The job required a great deal of his time and energy, the learning curve was steep, and Jerry had little time to acquire the skills of managing multi-million dollar projects. On the other hand, he did find that the leadership aspect did not differ much from that of a school environment. Pleasing the field staff was not much different from playgrounds and hallways full of children, as human nature does not change much with age. Field supervisors required the same encouragement and support as his classroom teachers, and the client demands resembled the unique and careful touch needed by parents. Jerry took to the new setting and its stresses quite naturally. Problem solving and conflict resolutions were nothing new to him, and he successfully treated each incident as he did when in his principal's chair.

Projects came and went, and the months passed quicker than Jerry could flip the pages on his calendar. He settled in, had become a lively addition to the office, and was often told that he brought with him a light that had long been missing from their building. He felt at home with the staff and had joyfully accepted that God had placed him where he belonged now, and where he would live out the rest of his working years. After another year of growth and sobriety, he and Maggie were confident in the stability of the career and began discussing the sale of their house and a permanent move to the city. They started their search for homes and surveying surrounding high schools in which to enroll their son, Allen, for his final two years. Jerry was back on top of his career. He and Maggie had fallen deeper in love than they could have ever imagined. Elaine was enjoying her college years, paid in full by an athletic scholarship, and the family was planning their reunion back under one roof. Everything appeared to be back on track and sailing on smooth waters towards a beautiful metaphoric sunset.

Now at this point, most readers would find it hard to believe that Jerry still had an emptiness in his heart. Even Jerry would wrestle with his feelings and ask himself how he could be so selfish to continue wanting more. In most of his bedtime prayers and conversations with the Lord, Jerry would ask forgiveness for feeling so unhappy and begged for a satisfied heart and the ability to appreciate all that had been given to him. However, it seemed the more he prayed, the worse the emptiness ate at his heart both day and night. What we too often fail to realize is that these passions, desires and empty holes that ache to be filled, are actually put there by no one else but the Father as a way to keep tugging on our heart and pulling us where He wants us to go.

Jerry's sleepless nights were simply caused by the few thousand adults, children and coworkers he had left behind. Whether he was two states away and making more money than he could shove in his pockets, it still did not resolve the fact that he had left some of the most important people of his life all believing that he had failed. Sure, being the typical small city of its kind, gossip spread and most knew where he was and what he was doing. However, there seemed to be another chapter that was missing, and Jerry had a burning aspiration to write those pages in order to bring closure to that book. The worst thing about it was the hopeless feeling of knowing that with what he had done to earn his termination, he would never have the opportunity to return to that life and reopen those pages again; at least not in the natural world where things make sense.

Over the last three years, Jerry and Dr. Robinson had remained in contact through sporadic holiday greeting cards, emails and the occasional short phone conversation. At times, Jerry would share how much he missed the students, but also accepted this chapter of his life was behind him and closed. With Dr. Robinson's typical response of awkward silence, Jerry understood it to be a concurrence of opinions. The phone calls or messages were for the purpose of keeping up with current events back home and sharing entertaining stories now and then, and the occurrences of their chats had become fewer and farther apart. They both had their own careers and their own families, and the busier they got, the harder it was to find time to touch base and catch up. So when Jerry answered his phone on that April morning and heard Dr. Robinson's voice on the other end, he was eager to sit down and spend a little extra time discussing the most recent developments back home. He was most excited to share his recent promotion and their plans to move the family to the city. Before he could even start to report his thrilling news, Dr. Robinson took control of the phone call and what he heard, sat Jerry straight down in his chair and then slid him back down on his knees.

"Are you ready to come home Jerry?" he asked. "The junior high school is struggling and losing its principal. The students and teachers need leadership like yours, and together we can turn this place around. Are you ready to come home where you belong?"

Jerry's silence on the other end now had Dr. Robinson guessing. The proposal was very intriguing since it offered him the miraculous chance to redeem himself and his reputation. Of course, the task of building a team that would defy the odds and take a failing school out of the trenches was even more attractive to him. Such challenges always got his blood boiling. On the other hand, the prospect of returning to the community, and especially the school system, scared the life out of Jerry. The thought of facing the judgement and condemnation of parents and townspeople caused a level of anxiety equal to sitting across the table from the hangman District Attorney and his gunman. To add to his dilemma, Jerry considered the point that his current place of employment had looked past his mistakes, given him a fresh start to a career and a gracious promotion in a record-breaking timeframe. To top it off, very few knew of Jerry's past in his new place of work and he had nothing hanging over his head. He questioned the possible reactions of his employers and whether resigning after such a short time was truly a manner in which he should repay them and show his gratitude for such a commitment.

He had only a short few days to make his decision since the school district was set to interview several candidates if Jerry did not accept. The predicament pulled Jerry in all directions. One would think that Maggie would be begging him to come home, but she too knew what was at stake and was hesitant to encourage a hasty decision. She wanted her husband home and by her side, but she also valued the happiness and security they had found, and feared losing it again if this "re-do" turned to disaster. Jerry's prayers for guidance did not seem to be yielding any great signs or words from his Father. He questioned God and asked if this door was genuine and of God's making, or if the new career and life for which Jerry had been working so hard was where he was to stay. The silence and absence of God's clear direction confused Jerry and brought him to the possible conclusion that maybe God was simply leaving that decision to Jerry and would be satisfied with his choice.

As parents, we all understand that in many cases, absolute silence is the best answer to our children's sporadic, confounding and absurd demands. The lack of response is far better than losing our tempers and saying what is really on our mind at that very moment. The stillness not only allows mothers and fathers the needed time to cool down, but also an opportunity for the son or daughter to rethink the phrasing of their demands and a little time for their words to rattle around in that head of theirs until they hear exactly how it sounded when it came out of their mouth. Well, while sitting in the next Sunday's worship service, Jerry got his answer for God's absolute silence. It took a sermon about Moses' message to the Israelites he was leading to the promised land for Jerry's words to rattle around his own head and for him to hear the selfish pride in his own prayers.

When you eat, get full, build nice houses, and settle down, and when your herds and your flocks are growing large, your silver and gold are multiplying, and everything you have is thriving, don't become arrogant, forgetting the LORD your God: the one who rescued you from the house of slavery; the one who led you through this vast and terrifying desert of poisonous snakes and scorpions, of cracked ground with no water; the one who made water flow for you out of a hard rock; the one who fed you manna in the wilderness, which your ancestors never experienced, in order to humble and test you, but in order to do good to you in the end.

> *Don't think to yourself, my own strength and abilities have produced all this prosperity for me. Remember the LORD your God!... But if you do, in fact, forget the LORD your God and follow other gods, serving and bowing down to them, I swear to you right now that you will be completely destroyed-all because you didn't obey the LORD your God's voice.*
>
> Deuteronomy 8: 12-20 (CEB)

It quickly became obvious to Jerry that the passion and burning inside his heart was of God's doing and the doubtful hesitation to follow it was caused by none other than the familiar whispers of the enemy. Jerry indeed had become arrogant and prideful, starting to think that his hard work and determination was yielding the prosperity that he was experiencing. With every word of the sermon that morning, he could hear the message spoken directly to him, reminding him of exactly who had rescued him from the slavery under the addiction, who provided the income for the food when it didn't seem like they were going to make it, and who had brought their marriage out of the wilderness. The very next day, and without any further hesitation, Jerry humbly submitted his letter of resignation and gave his two-week notice. Sitting across the desk from Mr. Copeland, Jerry was quite surprised to see that his boss was very understanding and supportive of Jerry's decision to be home with his family. He confirmed that they hated to see him leave, but at the same time admitted that individual and family needs should always supersede the needs of any business. As usual, Jerry had completely misjudged the intentions and reactions of others, and he began to recognize the need to curtail his habit of resorting to the unnecessary worrying of worst-case scenarios. Up to this point in his life, Jerry had seen blessing after blessing from God, and was starting to figure out that his acts of worrying was nothing less than gestures of doubt in the Lord God's promises.

That being said, Jerry was not so convinced when it came to his hometown community members and their willingness to accept and forgive his past. Before he left the small city, his closest friends and family had assured him they had not abandoned him. They vowed their support and unyielding friendship, no matter the cost. However, that did not account for the remaining few thousand who he had yet to face. He couldn't help thinking when the first serious discipline case hit his desk, he would be accused as a hypocrite for assessing any type of consequence on the child. He was concerned for his friend, Dr. Robinson, who would surely have to answer to those critics who would question his decision to place a known addict in the highest position of trust and responsibility over hundreds of students and their safety. As for the teachers, he questioned how many might reject his leadership, devalue his guidance and direction, and how long it would take before a crowd would demonstrate an all-out rebellion.

These concerns and self-developed prophesies of doom soon had Jerry questioning how he should open the first scene of this "part two" sequel. Like the pendulum in his office clock, Jerry swayed from one extreme to the other. On one hand, through his experiences in education, he had seen with his own eyes the results of leading with love and compassion, as well as the catastrophic fallout from ruling with a hammer. On the other hand, he contemplated if an iron fist would be the shocking factor needed to squash any thoughts of rebellion and autonomy. It would take only one example to set the bar and firmly display the absolute intolerance of any such anarchy.

Our Lord does not always answer our prayers or shine His light on our path through grand signs in the sky, a booming voice, or revealing scriptures from the Bible. Sometimes, God will use the most unimagined and discreet tools to stop us right in our tracks and receive His message loud and clear. The good Lord employs whatever or whoever it takes to touch our hearts and show us His will, if we are still enough to listen and obey. For Jerry, it was when aimlessly flipping through the hundreds of cable television channels and pausing for a moment to take another bite of his late night snack. By chance, coincidence, or divine intervention, the unintentional delay in rapid-fire channel changing landed on a documentary of the American Revolution and the suppression that led to the "shot heard around the world". After setting his half-eaten sandwich back on the plate, Jerry grabbed the remote control to continue his brainless search for entertainment, but instead found a slight interest in the narrator's description of the historic events that led up to the revolt. Within just a few short minutes of listening to the examples of outright tyranny that persuaded thousands of average colonial citizens to sacrifice their lives, the absurdity in Jerry's own consideration of an iron-fisted control became embarrassingly obvious to him. By no means would a Machiavellian style of governance prevent a rebellion, nor would it reunite a divided and self-directed school of students and staff of teachers. On the contrary, it would beckon the exact "spirit" that Jerry did not want to be attending that school any longer. It would actually invite rebellion and resentment, and would finish off an already sinking ship.

Opening week was quickly approaching, and Jerry's anxiety was building with each passing day. Spending another typical late night stare-a-thon at the ceiling above his bed, Jerry fought the doubts that began to creep back into his thoughts. He began to question his abilities and qualifications to lead the school after being away from the profession for so many years. Soon, his mind began to drift through the memories of his twisting and turning adventure that started in his teenage years and brought him to this very moment. With the recollection of each instance of God's miraculous intervention in his life, Jerry's anxiety slowly dissipated as he began realizing that never did he simply stumble upon his past God-given revelations and life lessons through some random coincidental chance, nor were they revealed to him without a purpose. In fact, they were preparing him for this very moment, and the purpose was far greater than any construction project that he left behind. However, in order for Jerry to fully serve out his purpose, he would have to find the ability to discern the voice of the enemy, and his destructive whispers of doubt, manipulation and deceit, and know when to stomp squarely on the serpent's head. There was no more confusion or guessing. Jerry knew what needed to be done at the school. First, they had to stop the ship from sinking, and that had to be accomplished before even thinking about turning the enormous vessel around.

The fundamental foundation of the junior high did not have a few holes or cracks that needed repairing. It did not require a little shoring up or remodeling. A couple of years prior, they had experienced a record high number of fights, drug usage, suspensions and expulsions. A foundational structure was literally non-existent, and what portions did exist, were still under reconstructive efforts. He and his staff definitely had their work cut out for them, and it was not going to be an easy task. Jerry and Dr. Robinson had the blueprints to their vision of the new footing, the list of materials required to construct it, and knew the very best "carpenter" to get the job done, which would be the help of Christ Himself. The stoutest and most fail proof of all foundations had to be fabricated using the fruits of the Spirit. Love, joy, peace, patience, kindness, goodness and faithfulness were the indispensable tools, and the absence of even just one of them would weaken the structure and cause it to crumble to the ground. The entire success of this mission was going to rest solely upon the ability to realign and synchronize the visions of an entire staff of teachers. several of whom were solidly indoctrinated in the rotten fruits of the opposing spirit.

Over the next month, Jerry began to recapture some of the passion he had left behind on that infamous day that changed his life. As he prepared his office for the upcoming year, he dedicated it to be a place where junior high students would feel safe and their circumstances would be heard and valued. By no means would he sweep student behavior under a rug, but at the same time, this office would no longer be known as the "dungeon" of the campus. Over the last three years, Jerry had recognized God's method of discipline, which included love, guidance and only the consequences necessary to promote a change of heart. It had changed Jerry's entire outlook on his discipline procedures as a principal and how he had once ruled the school with an unforgiving iron fist. He was now determined to take the time necessary with all misbehaving and misguided students to help them reflect on their lapse of good judgement, and to realize a more acceptable and appropriate action in the future. His entire focus would be to change their behavior by first leading them to a change of heart. Throughout the month, he and Dr. Robinson worked diligently to have everything in place for this refreshed and renewed establishment. The anticipation and excitement rekindled familiar emotions and enthusiasm he had experienced when he took the reins of the first school he ever led. Jerry was again ready to begin writing this new chapter in his life and eager for the chance to redeem himself and his renewed vision for the school.

Something else happened over that four-week period that strengthened Jerry's confidence and forced him to, once again, evaluate his prejudgments of others and their hearts. In order to lead the school through the improbable transformation, Jerry planned for battles on several fronts: winning the trust and respect of his staff; changing the hearts of the teachers towards the students; likewise changing the hearts of the students towards their teachers; and regaining the support and confidence of parents and community members. He envisioned his first re-encounter with the staff and townspeople to be played out in a large-group setting where he would look out upon a crowd of folded arms, suspicion-filled eyes, and doubtful shaking heads. The worst side effects caused by this anxiety were the triggers, of which James Corbett had frequently warned the class. These triggers were the familiar situations or conditions that would bring back intense desires to return to the addiction. Jerry never started taking his pain pills as a way to cope with stressful circumstances, but early on, as the addiction was taking hold of him, they soon did become a comforting crutch. Anyone who has taken an opiate medication knows the temporary false sense of confidence and contentment it brings. As stated before, true back pain was the original purpose for his introduction to the little white pills. However, with time, they became the key element to get Jerry through many of his daily stressors.

He knew that this was only the beginning of the stress and if he was going to survive without relapsing, he was going to have to find an escape plan and another coping mechanism. At home, Jerry dug through some boxes in the garage, dragged out his binder from the Calvary Recovery Center and began flipping through his notes, materials, and pages of his books. It wasn't long before he located his handwriting in bold letters "RESISTING RELAPSE!" There it was again, Mr. Corbett's instructions that led off with, and ended with, the importance of hiding behind Christ and relying on prayer and fellowship with other believers. Jerry shook his head at himself and admitted, once again he had allowed his work and circumstances to begin taking precedence over his faith and ongoing recovery. The pattern began to become very clear to him that whenever he let himself drift away from Christ, he allowed himself to drift right back into temptation. As long as Jerry stayed close to the Lord and relied on His guidance, he rarely even thought of the locked up demon that was just waiting for its chance to get out and cause havoc.

As for the anxiety-filled prophesy of Jerry's, it never did come to fruition. Instead, it seemed as if over the term of the next month, the Lord sent parents one-by-one to the school, to the grocery store, in the church, restaurants, and wherever else God desired. Each meeting was one of incredible grace and welcoming as parents expressed their joy and excitement for Jerry's return. Many nights, Maggie waited impatiently at home, while Jerry rushed to the supermarket with a short shopping list of the night's dinner items, but was unable to avoid the calls from down the bread aisle from a parent who simply wanted to express their delight in his return and share their desire to welcome him home.

By the final week of July, it had become clear to Jerry that his self-inflicted anxiety was just another attempt by the enemy to instill doubt and fear and, ultimately, derail God's plan of redemption and recovery. The condemnation and judgement by the parents and community he had so certainly expected, ended up being a battle he fought only in his mind. Once this was lifted off his shoulders, Jerry was able to refocus his battle plan and narrow his attention on what truly mattered. That was reconditioning a school of minds and hearts and helping them believe and see t they are all on the same team and can actually work together for one goal.

As the staff returned from their summer break, Jerry was once again reassured by their welcoming gestures and wishes of good will. His beginning of the year preparations were frequently interrupted by one teacher after another, stopping by his office to express their joy and relief that he answered the call to return. As each staff member would leave his office, Jerry would sit back and shake his head in astonishment with his Father's extraordinary ability to clear a road and soften the hearts of those in our paths. As the first day of school drew near, his anxiety was reduced to simple nervousness and the desire to lead the school in the direction God wanted it to go.

As for Dr. Robinson and whether he did indeed have to answer to any parents who doubted Jerry's abilities, no one will ever know. He was a man of Christian integrity, who would have never placed that information on Jerry's shoulders even if he had been fielding phone calls and concerns by the dozens. Instead, Dr. Robinson stood by Jerry's side every step of the way, giving him whatever was needed for his successful return. Together, they agreed upon what needed to continue changing at the school and lined up the necessary teacher training and support needed to make those changes.

The final Sunday night of summer had finally come, and Jerry found himself sitting behind his desk and watching the clock strike midnight. Whether he was ready or not, the time had come. The official school year was only seven hours away. Jerry bowed his head and asked the Father for the wisdom and constant guidance necessary to carry out what God had planned for the school and each of His precious children. He thanked the Lord for the countless blessings that had led up to this undeserved and unearned opportunity. If he had taken the time to call out each and every astonishing account of God's grace and mercy in his life, Jerry would have prayed straight through the night and into the daylight hours. Comforted with the fact that God knows our hearts and for what we are truly thankful, Jerry cut the prayer short. He ended with a final "thank you" for Maggie's, Elaine's and Allen's constant display of unconditional love, a major source of Jerry's strength and resilience, and for which, even if he spent the remainder of his life trying, he would never be able to repay.

LANIER T. NORTHRUP

The Most Difficult Mountain to Climb: Forgiveness

The school year started out like any other typical year; fast and busy. Students were on their best behavior as they sized up their teachers and cautiously welcomed newly arriving classmates. Last year's timid seventh graders were now the proud eighth grade royalty of the campus. The incoming 150 sixth graders resembled a litter of runt puppies just trying to stay out of sight and out of the way. As for the teachers, they were back on their familiar stages, reciting verbatim the exact opening act they had produced and performed so many times before. The same corny jokes, the same gripping life stories, the repetitious lists of "thou shall NOT, or else…." The identical course syllabi as each year before were again being passed out as if these students were the first to have ever been privileged to the highly confidential information. The honeymoon was in full swing, and Jerry was experienced enough to know that it was just a matter of time before his office would welcome the first unruly customers of the season. Parent requests, student schedules, teacher needs, and the daily tasks of managing a school took up every second of Jerry's time, and before he knew it, they were well into the second month of the semester.

As usual and right on time, the first wave of unruly students began to trickle into his office for one behavior reason or another. It did not take long for the teachers to begin seeing the "new" Jerry and his methods of student discipline. Jerry was no longer driven by the idea of enacting some ingenious form of emotionally painful punishment on a child as a means of seeking revenge for an act of disrespect. He now understood the value of mercy and the true purpose of discipline, and that is simply to lovingly guide a student towards a change of heart. Certainly, consequences are necessary and are not to be spared. However, the real change will happen when the child pays the natural and fair price in a dignified and respectful manner, rather than punished by one who is driven by an angry and revengeful heart. Genuine discipline is accomplished through conviction rather than condemnation. Condemnation is through a focus on the crime, where conviction is a focus on the solution. Condemnation is a focus on the punishment, where conviction is a focus on rewards of correcting the behavior. Condemnation leads to guilt and resentment, as conviction yields discovering the truth and leads to a change of heart. Jerry was living proof of our Father's unconditional love for His children, and an eyewitness to the fact that merciful discipline can change a life.

> *Know this, my dear brothers and sisters: everyone should be quick to listen, slow to speak, and slow to grow angry. This is because an angry person does not produce God's righteousness."*
>
> James 1:19 (CEB)

Of course, not all teachers and staff members were on board with Jerry's new approach to junior high behavioral management. He liked to think of the few rebels as the "Pharisee" teachers, who liked to appear holier than all and wanted every violating student to be punished to the full extent, and if still legal, would have probably preferred a public stoning. Even though these few teachers caused some difficulties for Jerry and the leadership team, the overall outcome proved to have quite the positive impact. Given a semester's timeframe, some remarkable transformations began to shine through the students' rough exteriors. Adolescents, who had continually resorted to swinging fists as a first means of resolving a disagreement, were now racing into the office to blow off their steam, in hopes Jerry or a member of the team could talk them down from the next fight. Others would come in and visit about a home issue that was causing them to lose focus in class. They would ask for a quiet day in solitary in order to silently work on their studies and avoid an awkward confrontation with a demanding teacher.

For the first time in his fifteen-year career in education, Jerry was building actual relationships with students and parents. Unlike the superficial interactions to which he had become so accustomed in his past, bonds of trust and respect began to form between all stakeholders. Jerry was dangerously getting real close to having a discussion that he had been avoiding for a long time, and that discussion was with himself. He had promised Mr. Corbett, "The day that I can find someone who is better off because of the mistakes I made, that will be the day that I consider even starting to forgive myself." It was starting to appear that much of what Jerry had learned from his mistakes was starting to be used for the good of others. Even though he played it off in his head and heart as still not being enough to justify his self-forgiveness, he would soon to be placed right in the position where he could no longer ignore it.

By springtime, the teen-age activity level was definitely on the rise but was still amazingly calm and peaceful. This lack of anticipated mayhem appeared to be too much to stand for the last few Pharisee-minded teachers. In their frustration, they went out in full force, catching and reporting every infraction of young-love display of affection and one-second student tardiness to their seats. It had become a normal and expected routine to be visited by the two or three unfortunate daily targets, so seeing the disappointed face of the next student did not surprise Jerry as he entered the office and handed him a note from the teacher. Jerry told the boy to have a seat while he began reading the letter that stated a concern with the student's recent behavior. Jerry took notice of the watery and constricted pupils and struck a conversation with the young man regarding the day's events. He quickly detected a lethargic mannerism that was unusual for the normally talkative and borderline hyperactive youngster. Jerry asked the young man how his day was going, inquired if he was feeling ill, and began to delve into the boy's recent activities, which soon extracted the disturbing truth.

Any typical fourteen-year-old would have lied and denied any wrongdoing, and blamed his behavior on something such as a lack of sleep caused by domestic troubles at home. However, in an act of completely surrendered trust, the boy seemingly leaped at the opportunity to come clean and shockingly opened his soul to Jerry. In what appeared to be a genuine cry for help, he began to portray an extremely familiar progression of body language that Jerry could recall as if it were yesterday. From an upright and confident posture, the teenager slowly melted into a bent-over and broken boy. With his chin to his chest and his forehead in his hands, he spoke through his folded palms. He addressed Jerry by his last name, said he was in trouble and did not know what to do, and after a short pause, he spilled his soul. The troubled teen confessed to the year-long pilfering of countless pill bottles from the cabinets of family members, friends, and any others he could get his hands on, and ingesting them on a regular basis. He then pulled out a plastic sandwich bag from deep in his pants pocket and laid it on Jerry's desk. Almost paralyzed, Jerry stared at a plastic bag full of the same white pills that had almost taken and destroyed his life four short years before, and flashes of the horrors replayed in his head. He looked up from the desk and into the teary eyes of the teenager, immediately reaching out and embracing the boy as if he was holding on to a younger version of himself. Jerry had not shed a tear since the day he hunched over in his truck outside of the courthouse, and this moment broke the dry streak. The two stood in the middle of the office, sharing silent tears as Jerry held the boy's bowed head against his shoulder. He dreaded the phone calls that he was about to make as he knew too well the road on which the teen was about to embark and wished it on no one. However, he also knew that if the young man stood even the slightest chance to break free from the evil grips of the overpowering addiction, it would be determined in what transpired over the course of that afternoon and determined whether the young man left with a heart full of despair or a mustard seed of hope.

Oblivious to the reason for being called to the school headquarters, the single mother was the first to arrive. Except for the occasional tardiness to class, the teenager was not known for stirring up problems at school. The surprise request for the mom to leave her place of employment and come directly to the office had her quite bewildered. Jerry welcomed her to take a seat next to her son, who sat holding his head buried in his hands and fearing the absolute worse. As Jerry broke the news, the mother's shoulders began to slump and tears filled her eyes. An absolute sense of horror and hopelessness had overtaken the loving, but out-of-touch mom. Just as Jerry had sat at his dining room table a few years before, the teenage boy could not bring himself to look his mother in the eyes and see the pain he was causing her. As they both sat staring down at their feet, Jerry gave her a few awkward seconds of stillness to collect her thoughts and then he took a seat beside her.

He had no idea what to expect from the shocked and dazed mom. Part of him braced for a rebuttal of outright denial, as another side of him waited for the long expected accusation of pure hypocrisy and the defensive grilling of how Jerry could justify disciplining a student for the same crime of which he was guilty. Out of her silence, she finally lifted her head, reached toward Jerry and tightly grabbed his hands. Looking him deep in the eyes, and fighting her trembling voice, she exclaimed with an almost pleading tone that she was fully aware of Jerry's past struggles and at one time was not sure what to think about him returning as a principal. However, now she had no more doubts and knew that because of his past, Jerry was the only one who could help guide her and her son to recovery. At that instant, the exact same indescribable and overwhelming warming feeling of calm, strength and determination that saved Jerry from his planned head-on collision, started in Jerry's core and spread throughout his entire body. It was at that moment Jerry clearly saw the full circle God had so carefully orchestrated, and the true meaning of *God works all things together for good for the ones who love God, for those who are called according to his purpose.*

As expected, the meetings with the police and other school officials lasted several hours. As the late afternoon unfolded, Jerry could recognize the seeds of hope growing inside the mother and son's hearts. Their looks of despair and helplessness slowly evolved into expressions of faith and confidence. As the two left the office that evening, Jerry watched as the mother walked down the hallway with her arm around her son. As the door closed behind them, he turned around to head back towards his office and, finally, took his first step up the steep slope of the mountain of self-forgiveness.

LANIER T. NORTHRUP

What is Recovery?

When you really get down to the details of recovery, we definitely make it more complicated than it truly is. The facts are the facts. Those of us who have been addicted to whatever it may be, can tell you that the simple fact is; we just cannot stop! We have tried everything under our own power, but they have been only futile attempts to kill a giant who just laughs at our weapons. We hear the tragic stories over and over again about how fellow addicts are back in addiction recovery for the fourth or fifth time, and eventually pass away from the inevitable overdose. Every so often, we catch a rare success story of a former addict who is now dedicated to helping others break free from the chains. The stories are few and far between and our media fails to share some of the very important details and common factors among the success stories and failed attempts.

We have to face the fact that if we were unable to break the addiction by ourselves, then what value can be added from some additional psychology lessons and self-help advice. The answer is, very little, if any. We are still relying on our own strength, intelligence and willpower to withstand vicious attacks from a world that we cannot see or even imagine that exists. Our flesh failed to fight the battle once before, and it is going to continue to fail every time we try to fight it alone. Sure, there are some cases where an addict has been "cured" by the use of other medicines or therapies. However, all that accomplished was to substitute one substance for another and put a leash on the wild beast who will start chewing on that rope.

Just as any disease is cured, the root cause must be attacked and killed. There are many incurable illnesses that attack humans every day. Doctors are simply limited to treating the symptoms and trying to slow down the effects in order to prolong the patient's life. If we treat the disease of addiction with only medications and/or self-help psychological tactics, we are treating it the same as all other incurable diseases. We simply put a leash on the beast for a while, knowing that when and if it breaks free, there is very little hope the second time around. We were not psychologically strong enough to kill the beast on our own the first time, so what makes you think we can kill it on the second go around?

In agreement with the Twelve Step Program, the first step is the most vital to anyone's success. Whether you are addicted to drugs, alcohol, gambling, pornography, food, or any other life-damaging substance or activity, you must be willing to start at the ground floor. There is absolutely no way to circumvent the necessity of seeing and accepting your current state in the true mess that it is. Then, it is imperative that you verbally admit what you see, and that is your life is out of control and admit that you are powerless to the drug and that your life has become unmanageable.

For years, Jerry was able to see the truth of his addiction. However, his unwillingness to verbally state it to another fellow human being is what led him to the bottom and what leads most to their eventual death. Once we verbally confess and speak our addiction to a fellow human being, an unexplainable power is released. We instantly have the vision and courage to do what needs to be done in order to begin fighting the demon. This is exactly why the demon whispers constant lies to you in attempts to keep your addiction top secret. You know the lies, they sound something very similar to this. "Sure, there are people who might have a suspicion of your problem, but if you admit an addiction, they will all lose respect for you because you are showing your weakness. Just keep it private and you can quit anytime you want."

Once you have spoken the words of confession, it will have destroyed the ability of the enemy to use these lies as a weapon against you. Immediately following your confession, you must realize your state of vulnerability and the absolute need for God to step in. It is at this point that Satan will recognize that he is in danger of losing his grip on you, and, he will begin to strike even harder. I cannot stress enough the outright necessity of having the one true God at your side during this time. It is not a suggestion or a choice. It is an absolute must.

No one who is tested should say, "God is tempting me!" This is because God is not tempted by any form of evil, nor does he tempt anyone. Everyone is tempted by their own cravings; they are lured away and enticed by them. Once those cravings conceive, they give birth to sin; and when sin grows up, it gives birth to death.

Don't be misled, my dear brothers and sisters. Every good gift, every perfect gift, comes from above. These gifts come down from the Father, the creator of the heavenly lights, in whose character there is no change at all. He chose to give us birth by his true word, and here is the result: we are like the first crop from the harvest of everything he created.

James 1: 13-18 (CEB)

LANIER T. NORTHRUP

Absolute Necessity of Trusting God Through Recovery

At the risk of losing your attention to the redundancy of facts already stated earlier, it still must be stated and emphasized to the fullest. We do not have a choice of who God is, His plan for us, and His methods of governing the universe. You may find yourself in disagreement with your personal interpretation or perception of God's will or His actions, but contrary to your belief system, God is not going to change in order to satisfy your wishes. There are no alternatives, loopholes, or substitutes for the truth. We have two choices and that is final. We can follow Satan's lies and deception and be led down his road of destruction. That road takes us only one place, and that is where God will be sentencing Satan for eternity. If we choose to follow Satan's lies and lust for earthly pleasures, we follow him straight to hell. Satan's lies include all of your justifications for your choices up to this point. These lies include your belief that since you are generally a good person with a good heart, God will save you from hell and reserve a spot in heaven for you. Unfortunately, that belief cannot be further from the truth, for it is plainly written that our works cannot and will not earn our way to salvation because we are all guilty of breaking God's laws.

All have sinned and fall short of God's glory, but all are treated as righteous freely by his grace because of a ransom that was paid by Christ Jesus.
Romans 3: 23-24 (CEB)

No matter how many good deeds we complete on this earth, none will earn our way to salvation. The only way to salvation is through the one and only who did satisfy God's laws and was sacrificed for our sake. When we accept that Christ was sacrificed for our sins and took our place on the cross, we then will have our names written in the Scroll of Life.

God is the one who saved and called us with a holy calling. This wasn't based on what we have done, but it was based on his own purpose and grace that he gave us in Christ Jesus before time began. Now his grace is revealed through the appearance of our savior, Christ Jesus. He destroyed death and brought life and immortality into clear focus through the good news.

2 Timothy 1: 9-10 (CEB)

Unfortunately, because we fear that the will of God may not match our selfish plans for our own lives, we resist the gift of salvation offered to us in Christ's outstretched hands on the cross. Many of us are afraid that if we do accept Christ's sacrifice, and surrender our will to the Lord, God will rob us of our earthly pleasures. However, because of our innate knowledge of and belief in God, our conscience forces us to accept the existence of an almighty being. Consequently, we invent an imaginary god who governs from a distance, changes with the times, looks beyond our choices to ignore his commandments, and gives us a free pass to paradise because we helped a few less fortunate people in our lives. The irony of the whole thing is that Satan sits right beside you and helps you invent every detail of this fabricated father of the universe. He will even make sure you make it to church every Sunday to worship this nonexistent king of the clouds. As long as you are not worshipping the one true God, Satan knows you are his and will be his forever. He is confident in his ownership of you due to your choice to rely on your works to enter heaven instead of Christ's sacrifice for you.

> *This Jesus is the stone you builders rejected; he has become the cornerstone! Salvation can be found in no one else. Throughout the whole world, no other name has been given among humans through which we must be saved.*
>
> Acts 4: 11-12 (CEB)

Unfortunately, since you have chosen to be judged by your works or what you have done, rather than accept the gift of God's grace, Satan has no doubt that you will be joining him for eternity.

Then I saw a great white throne and the one who is seated on it. Before his face both earth and heaven fled away, and no place was found for them. I saw the dead, the great and the small, standing before the throne, and scrolls were opened. Another scroll was opened too; this is the scroll of life. And the dead were judged on the basis of what was written in the scrolls about what they had done. The sea gave up the dead that were in it, and Death and the Grave gave up the dead that were in them, and people were judged by what they had done. Then Death and the Grave were thrown into the fiery lake. This, the fiery lake, is the second death. Then anyone whose name wasn't found written in the scroll of life was thrown into the fiery lake.

In order to fully grasp this concept, you must first understand the basic and fundamental, elementary-level relationship between our Heavenly Father and Satan. First of all, they are not equals who sit on their thrones and battle each other in a chess game of angels and demons. God created everyone and everything, including Satan. Therefore, God has ultimate power over Satan and his demons. When Satan or his minions even hear the name of Jesus Christ, they flee in fear of the Almighty and His Son.

But he gives us more grace. This is why it says, God stands against the proud, but favors the humble. Therefore, submit to God. Resist the devil, and he will run away from you. Come near to God, and he will come near to you.

James 4: 6-8 (CEB)

Secondly, we as humans are powerless to Satan and his demons. None of our self-help books and therapy is a match for the powers of darkness. Likewise, the powers of darkness are no match for the unfathomable powers of God Almighty. The only sensible conclusion is we must have God fight these battles for us and the only way that can be accomplished is by surrendering our will to His will and allowing Him to take over His rightly spot in our lives; that of our Lord and King. However, because of the gift of free will, we have to request God's help in removing Satan and his demons from our lives.

Once you have admitted you need help and have called on the only true God that can help, it is time to stock up on your weapons and tactics to be able to fight off the inevitable attacks and attempts to take you back. As stated earlier, these satanic attacks are not just for the sake of stealing your soul back from God. They have the sole purpose of stopping you from the possibility of helping save countless other souls from the same torturous demise. Satan will have a motive behind his fight for you, and even on your strongest day, your personal strength is only useless and pathetic. Ironically, Satan might even let you "win" a few battles just so you begin to build a false sense of security and pride in your own abilities. While allowing you to have some personal victory, he is letting your pride build and your need for God to diminish. Then, at the right time and the right circumstances, he will strike, and your pride and false sense of self-security will crumble under his first blow.

Therefore, humble yourselves under God's power so that he may raise you up in the last day. Throw all your anxiety onto him, because he cares about you. Be clearheaded. Keep alert. Your accuser, the devil, is on the prowl like a roaring lion, seeking someone to devour. Resist him, standing firm in the faith. Do so in the knowledge that your fellow believers are enduring the same suffering throughout the world. After you have suffered for a little while, the God of all grace, the one who called you into his eternal glory in Christ Jesus, will himself restore, empower, strengthen, and establish you. To him be power forever and always. Amen.

1 Peter 5: 6-11 (CEB)

In order to truly resist the temptations that Satan will throw at you, you must be in a daily walk with the Lord. Just as Jerry recognized the undeniable pattern in his inconsistent walk with the Lord, your resistance will weaken every time you drift away from a total reliance on the Father. Just as importantly, you must surround yourself with other believers and others who are fighting the same battle. It is understood that you cannot choose your coworkers or family. However, you can choose with whom you spend your free time and the influences they have on you. You know very well that you are powerless to the temptations and cravings. If it were not so, you would not be in this position to begin with. So, when the temptations begin and the flaming arrows of the enemy start to fly, you must run as fast as you can to those who share your faith and into the arms of the Lord.

Run away from adolescent cravings. Instead, pursue righteousness, faith, love, and peace together with those who confess the Lord with a clean heart.
2 Timothy 2:22 (CEB)

One of the most difficult fights to handle are the ones that we don't see. Those are the spiritual battles that happen around us at all times that our natural eyes are unable to see. For the beginning believer, this topic of discussion usually causes some discomfort, as well as very common reaction of disbelief and even sarcasm. The young Christian will accept the existence of God and even the death of His son Jesus as a payment for our sins. However, as soon as we mention the supernatural or spiritual realm, we tend to disregard it as "hocus pocus" and refuse to acknowledge the realities around us. Once again, this is exactly where the enemy wants us; oblivious to his games and torments caused by his demons, blaming the negative whispers in our ears on an emotional disorder, and attempting to fight it with medications or self-help books and therapists.

The entire purpose of God's laws, or Ten Commandments, was for His people to realize that we are completely incapable of upholding the demands. Therefore, we become completely reliant upon His Son, Jesus, for the forgiveness of falling short, to help us uphold the laws as we live our lives, and to provide the grace and forgiveness when we continue to stumble. Whether this seems too simple a solution or if it's simply our pride that will not allow us to accept the truth, the problem is that most of us refuse this free gift, choosing instead to fight a lifelong, torturous war we cannot win on our own. The emptiness in our hearts tells us there is something or someone missing. Instead of searching for the One by whom the void was created to be filled, we choose to cover it up with medications, drugs, alcohol, or physical relationships, but never satisfy the desolation and vacancy.

On the other hand, once you do finally choose to fill that void with Christ, there is an instant peace that overtakes your heart and a sense of wholeness that fills your soul. It is at this point that every truth you have read or heard from God's written word begins to make sense. It is when the true meaning of the words "faith, love, and joy" become clear and you realize that you had never truly experienced any one of them.

Jesus responded, "I assure you that if you have faith and don't doubt, you will not only do what was done to the fig tree. You will even say to this mountain, 'Be lifted up and thrown into the lake.' And it will happen. If you have faith, you will receive whatever you pray for."

Matthew 21: 21-22 (CEB)

God is love, and those who remain in love remain in God and God remains in them. This is how love has been perfected in us, so that we can have confidence on the Judgment Day, because we are exactly the same as God is in this world. There is no fear in love, but perfect love drives out fear, because fear expects punishment. The person who is afraid has not been made perfect in love. We love because God first loved us.

1 John 4: 16-19 (CEB)

When he arrives home, he calls together his friends and neighbors, saying to them, 'Celebrate with me because I've found my lost sheep.' In the same way, I tell you, there will be more joy in heaven over one sinner who changes both heart and life than over ninety-nine righteous people who have no need to change their hearts and lives.

Luke 15: 6-7 (CEB)

It is at this point, and at no time before, that you begin to understand why an attempt at addiction recovery without The Trinity leading, guiding and protecting, is most often times a futile effort. Once you have experienced the Father's touch of love and you have felt the unexplainable joy that has been missing from your life, the act of placing your complete faith in your Savior is no longer a mystery. Even though this new life is indescribable in words, the entire picture of the world and our existence makes perfect sense. It is also at this point when you have honestly conquered Step 3. If you are going to turn your will and life over to the care of a god, it only seems sensible to turn it over to the one true living God, and not to some fabricated and imaginary, nonexistent idea. You would not consider for even a second the thought of suggesting that you leave a newborn baby under the care of an imaginary friend for a week rather than a real-life, certified, trusted babysitter. Why then, would you trust your eternity to such a fabrication of your imagination?

Forgiveness; It's Not Something to "Find" in Your Heart

Once you have made the choice to place your addiction and your life in the hands of God, the Father, the remainder of the steps also begin to become crystal clear. The act of asking for and giving forgiveness is not an easy task for the human heart. We tend to want to hold onto anger and resentment toward someone who has hurt us or caused pain to someone close to us. We live under the false pretense that we are punishing the offender by refusing forgiveness and hoping for some sort of vengeance. On the contrary, what we don't realize is that our deep resentment and refusal to forgive is hurting nobody but ourselves. While we are suffering sleepless nights, anxiety-filled days, and months since we can remember the last time we smiled or felt any hint of joy, our offender is completely unaffected. There are two rewards found in forgiveness: the first, of course, is found in following God's commandment to us that we shall forgive and love our enemies as Christ has loved us.

> *Don't let any foul words come out of your mouth. Only say what is helpful when it is needed for building up the community so that it benefits those who hear what you say. Don't make the Holy Spirit of God unhappy—you were sealed by him for the day of redemption. Put aside all bitterness, losing your temper, anger, shouting, and slander, along with every other evil. Be kind, compassionate, and forgiving to each other, in the same way God forgave you in Christ.*
>
> Ephesians 4: 29-32 (CEB)

The second reward we earn from forgiveness is the relief we enjoy when we let go of the immense burden of resentment and anger. As soon as we hand over our cares and pain to the Lord and trust Him to serve justice as He sees fit, peace and happiness can once again fill our hearts where we had been crowding it out with vengeance and rage.

Don't pay back anyone for their evil actions with evil actions, but show respect for what everyone else believes is good.

If possible, to the best of your ability, live at peace with all people. Don't try to get revenge for yourselves, my dear friends, but leave room for God's wrath. It is written, Revenge belongs to me; I will pay it back, says the Lord.

Romans 12: 17-19 (CEB)

Revenge is my domain, so is punishment-in-kind, at the exact moment their step slips up, because the day of their destruction is just around the corner; their final destiny is speeding on its way!

Deuteronomy 32: 35 (CEB)

Arriving at this revelation is the turning point of a person's entire recovery. If you do not understand the meaning, purpose and value behind the action of forgiveness, then every one of the other steps are worthless and of no resolve. Forgiveness is the complete foundation and the entire hope upon which we rest our faith. It is the sole reason that Christ willfully allowed us to torture him, nail his hands and feet to a cross, and ultimately kill him. It was for nothing more and nothing less than to receive the punishment in our place so that we can be forgiven if we so choose.

It is not a revelation of some grand declaration to state that we are not God, nor can we walk the earth in perfection as He did through His Son, Jesus Christ. We will all make mistakes, some errors are made inadvertently, and many we commit with absolute ill-hearted intent. As the Apostle Paul wrote to the Romans, "*All have sinned and fall short of God's glory.*" In other words, contrary to what some believe, nobody is perfect. We all have broken God's laws and will continue to break His laws.

Some people may ask, "And, what's the big deal about that?" The big deal is that the only path to Heaven is through perfection; no broken laws, 100 percent accuracy for life, batting 1.000 from birth to death. Therefore, none of us is capable of passing that exam, as a 99% grade is still a failing grade. However, God has given us a promise and that promise is that *all are treated as righteous freely by his grace because of a ransom that was paid by Christ Jesus. Through his faithfulness, God displayed Jesus as the place of sacrifice where mercy is found by means of his blood. He did this to demonstrate his righteousness in passing over sins that happened before, during the time of God's patient tolerance. He also did this to demonstrate that he is righteous in the present time, and to treat the one who has faith in Jesus as righteous.*

Romans 3:24-26 (CEB)

If you are a Christian, this is God's promise on which you firmly stand. This is the certainty that wakes you in the morning and allows you to sleep peacefully at night. This is the covenant on which you lean and in which you place every ounce of hope and faith. Without this promise of God's forgiveness through Christ, there is absolutely no optimism and the whole purpose and outcome of life is one of despair and doom. As a Christian, you understand that you are incapable of living the sinless life and, therefore, have humbly accepted this undeserved and unearned gift of mercy and compassion from our Father.

The question then is one that hopefully leads you through self-reflection, and ultimately allowing you to continue past Step 4. If I accept and rest my eternal life on God's gift of forgiveness through the sacrifice of His Son, Jesus Christ, what then justifies my hesitation and unwillingness to offer that same gift to someone who has offended me? Are my personal laws of greater importance than those of God? Is my forgiveness of greater significance than that of the Father? Or, is it simply that I am caught in the most absurd act of hypocrisy?

When you realize that forgiveness is the basis of all healing, and it is the greatest demonstration of love one can offer, then we are ready to begin taking the next steps in our recovery. If you expect to have God remove, forgive and wash clean all of your character defects, sins and shortcomings, you must first let go of the resentment you have toward others' character defects, sins and shortcomings.

The absolute truth is written all throughout the Bible and spelled out very clearly. God has given us the one and only path to forgiveness and His kingdom. There are no loopholes, exclusions, or side note clarifications in the contract. He gives us the law that was originated through The Ten Commandments for us to understand what God's expectations are. If we are to rely on our works and efforts to earn our way into heaven, then we must be able to meet the expectations of that law with 100 percent accuracy, and without a single blemish or mistake. Because, if you have broken even one law, then you have broken them all. Once we realize that we are completely incapable of upholding God's law to His desired perfection, we then arrive at the understanding that we need God's mercy and forgiveness. That forgiveness is available to every one of us and is a free gift. However, that forgiveness and salvation is offered in one way, and only one way.

You are saved by God's grace because of your faith. This salvation is God's gift. It's not something you possessed. It's not something you did that you can be proud of. Instead, we are God's accomplishment, created in Christ Jesus to do good things. God planned for these good things to be the way that we live our lives.
Ephesians 2: 4-10 (CEB)

Jesus answered, "I am the way, the truth, and the life. No one comes to the Father except through me. If you have really known me, you will also know the Father. From now on you know him and have seen him."
John 14: 6-7 (CEB)

As a ransom for our sins, God sent His Son Jesus to be the ultimate sacrifice, or to be punished and die as a payment for our mistakes and our sins. By Christ's suffering and death, our sins were paid for and would no longer have to be answered for on judgement day. To whom did this sacrifice have to be paid? you might ask. To God, Himself. It was a payment that would satisfy His own perfect laws and nature. So, now that God has completed His ultimate plan for our salvation, by sacrificing His only Son as the ransom to satisfy His own laws, why in the world would He all of a sudden decide to change His mind just to appease and satisfy our stubborn denial? Exactly; He would not. If he did, it would make the suffering and death of His Son be for absolutely no reason. God did not sacrifice His Son as just "one of several ways" to heaven. It is the ONLY way to heaven.

> *So now there isn't any condemnation for those who are in Christ Jesus. The law of the Spirit of life in Christ Jesus has set you free from the law of sin and death. God has done what was impossible for the Law, since it was weak because of selfishness. God condemned sin in the body by sending his own Son to deal with sin in the same body as humans, who are controlled by sin. He did this so that the righteous requirement of the Law might be fulfilled in us.*
>
> Romans 8: 2-4 (CEB)

The only thing asked of us individually is to humble our self, admit we are a sinner and cannot uphold His law, accept the fact that without Christ's sacrifice, we would be doomed to hell, and then repent and live the rest of our life guided by Christ and The Holy Spirit. Does this mean that you then live a perfect life? Absolutely not. However, our walk with the Lord helps us get closer and closer to perfection each day. When we do trip up and commit a sin, it is covered and erased by the gift of grace that was given to us at the cross. It is the gift that we did not deserve, yet it is simply given under God's unconditional love.

If you have genuinely taken these steps with a true and honest heart, you have just made the decision that has completely changed your eternity. If you truly admitted you are a sinner and cannot uphold the laws of God through your own works. If you realized that because of this, you are hopelessly at the mercy of God in order to save you from an eternity with the enemy. If you realized the only hope you do have is through the gift of forgiveness that God gave you by sacrificing His Son, Jesus Christ. If you chose to accept this gift of pure grace you did not earn or deserve, and chose to live the rest of your life with the risen Jesus Christ as your Lord, Savior and guide. Congratulations! You, my friend have just caused a celebration in heaven that you can't even imagine! The very best part about it is that all of your sins are now listed on the next page of this book, and those sins will be the ones held against you on judgement day

Yes, that's correct. Absolutely nothing is on that page! And that is because when you do accept the gift of salvation that God gave to you, Christ's blood has washed it clean and your Father no longer sees your mistakes, sins and shortcomings. He sees His Son in you. He sees perfection!

At this very moment, your doubt in the previous statement is beginning to rise. Your thoughts are turning to all of the horrible things you have done to others, with others, and to yourself. You are thinking of all of the thefts, lies and tricks you played on those you love in order to get your hands on your next high. On top of it all, there is a voice that is telling you this all sounds great and wonderful, but you have done too much. You have gone too far to be forgiven. "This forgiveness is for those who have not done the things I have done".

Now you are even more perplexed because that is exactly what is going through your mind, and you are wondering how your thoughts could be written right there in front of you. It's because Satan is so predictable and never changes his methods. The same old tricks he has used in the past are the same lies and misdirection he still uses today. The enemy will do and say whatever he can to whisper those doubts in your ear in his last efforts to stop you from leaving his grip on you. The jealousy and hatred is eating away at his core right this moment. He is squirming and screaming at the top of his lungs behind you, wanting so desperately for you to turn back to him so he can finish destroying you.

While standing in front of you, with His hand stretched out, is Christ with his open arms, ready to take you home where you belong. Ready to show you a life of freedom and clarity. Ready to teach you little by little how to grow closer to Him. Ready to take every one of your mistakes, your poor decisions, and your trespasses, so God can work all things together for good for the ones who love God, for those who are called according to his purpose.

Making the choice to allow Christ access to your heart gives you the strength and ability to do what you could never do on your own, and that is to earnestly forgive others for their trespasses against you. It is through these acts of forgiveness that now allow you to begin your quest into Step 4.

There is no way to gauge or even predict the amount of time you might spend climbing Steps 4 through 7. Just as the phases of grief are managed at different rates for each individual, so is the process of forgiveness. Each of us will have to come to terms with a wide variety of painful trespasses to which we fell victim. Some of us are still holding on to a teenage love affair that was split up by a jealous classmate. Once we realize the offender probably doesn't even remember what he or she did, we can come to grips with the fact that holding a grudge is definitely hurting only ourselves. However, it may not be so easy to let go of instances of abuse, long term bullying, and the ultimate pain of losing a loved one at the hands of another human being.

One of the most inaccurate and misguided words that come from the mouth of counselors, psychologists and well-meaning friends, is the statement that "you must find it in your heart to forgive." Forgiveness is not something lost or hiding in the deep pit of your heart and can only to be found if you go searching for it. The vacancy in your heart is a real thing. It is your choice what you fill it with, and what you fill it with will determine whether your heart is capable of forgiveness. Once again, this is not the job for some self-help guru or a fabricated greater power. Indeed, there is validity in being able to talk to fellow believers and the role it plays in the healing process. However, the process of forgiveness is a long one for many people, and the constant fellowship with The Holy Spirit and immersion in the word of God, is the only way to battle your way through it. Just remember this; time does not exist to God. Therefore, the amount of time it takes you to work through the process of forgiveness is irrelevant to your

Father. As long as you are growing, and God knows your heart to be true to the mission, His love is enduring.

Empty the Trash

The next three steps of the journey begin the cleansing of our conscience and heart. Once we have let go of our resentment towards others, we can begin asking for forgiveness from others, and to lay those sins at the foot of the cross where they belong.

Once an addict has made his list of those hurt by our actions, the very thought of approaching those people and confessing our trespasses creates an anxiety equal to none ever experienced before. The majority of that anxiety is generated directly by the whispers of the enemy who desperately wants to block your path. Hate, discontent, and resentment are some of Satan's most powerful weapons used to separate us from God. The last thing he wants us to do is give our foe a reason to forgive and begin healing. Therefore, the more lies and misguidance he can throw your way, the better chance he has of diverting your mission and giving you justification for avoiding what will not only break your addiction, but more importantly, seal your eternity.

Once you have stepped over the line of intimidation and anxiety for the first time and experience the freedom and release that comes with making amends, it becomes an addiction in itself. With every hug, handshake and tear, the lifetime of trash that has been collecting in your soul begins to empty, and the load that is removed is unexplainable.

As you walk through this step of recovery, another amazing epiphany is reached and a whole new world appears before your eyes and in your heart.

One of Jerry's biggest fears was facing his brothers, sister and parents as he attempted to make his amends. Not only had he swiped a few pills out of their medicine cabinets, but he also passively allowed them to be suspect of other innocent family members and friends for the missing meds. As he humbly met or talked with each one, only forgiveness and love were offered in return. Just like the father of the prodigal son, each were simply happy to have the real Jerry back in their lives.

The life-changing epiphany that struck Jerry deep in his heart was when he finally began to imagine and sense just the first drop of God's unending shower of love and forgiveness that He has for all of His children. If our family members, who are only capable of conditional human love, can so freely offer him forgiveness and welcome him home with such open arms, then how much more forgiveness is freely offered from our Father who loves divinely and unconditionally?

Understanding this unconditional and free love offered by the Father, allows us to begin letting go of our fears of rejection by the unforgiving. Whether those we have hurt are as ready to forgive as Jerry's family was, it does not stop us from taking that uncomfortable and intimidating step of asking for that forgiveness. The mercy and compassion may not be instant, but through your step of faith, the process of healing is allowed to start. Your closet begins to empty, and your shoulders begin to bear less and less weight.

Once the trash has been taken out and the closet is clean, you will discover the fact that you will want no bones to begin piling up ever again. We are human and living on this earth, which is consumed with selfish temptations all around us. Keeping your trash empty does not suggest living a perfect life by any means. What is asked of us is to live in Steps 10 through 12 for the remainder of our lives.

Once you have successfully climbed your way through the first nine steps, you will find what seemed to be an emotionally draining and humbling adventure, has actually cleansed and revitalized your entire being. There is absolutely no schedule or timeframe in which to complete your first nine steps. Each and every one of us will take these steps at our own rates and when God knows we are ready to take each one. Whatever your timeline, upon the completion of the ninth step, the final three are concurrent and a life-long walk with the Lord.

The unexplainable freedom that is enjoyed by those who have emptied their personal trash cans, is one that you will never want to lose. Maintaining your closet will be a natural action that will take very little effort on your behalf. You will have a burning desire to immediately admit any wrongdoing and ask for forgiveness, as even one little bone in the closet will be unacceptable to your new standards.

It is also at this point that your personal relationship with Jesus Christ will have become real. Many will no longer understand you, but will want to know where and how you have found your new joy. Some will desire and welcome your story and testimony. While others will desire to pull you back into the bucket of crabs in order to justify their unwillingness to even consider taking the first step. It is only in your walk with the Lord that you will be able to resist the old triggers and temptations. It is also through this relationship that you will be able to clearly see the truths in life and differentiate between those who are genuine in their wish to help you succeed and those who want only to drag you back under and join their miserable company. Most importantly, this real relationship with your Savior will lead to your instinctive desire for the knowledge of, and the willingness to follow His will for your life.

Steps 10 and 11 go hand-in-hand, as we are only able to maintain a personal relationship with our Lord Jesus when we are not holding on to unforgiven and hidden trash in our closets. By immediately righting our wrongs and not allowing any bones to pile up, we are able to stay in a closer walk with our Savior and able to clearly hear His direction. Likewise, through our closer walk with the Lord, we are given the power to avoid creating trash or bones to begin with. But when we do stumble, and we will, we also know that God's gracious gift of mercy is waiting for us with His arms wide open.

LANIER T. NORTHRUP

Trust and Obey God's Will and Plans for You

Just remember, after completing the final steps, the battle is not over. It will continue as long as you have a heartbeat and are a threat to the enemy. Satan will continue to send others in attempts to disrupt your path. He will relentlessly whisper his lies and deceitfulness, hoping to pull you off track. His most successful lie is convincing us that we have gone too far and have either sinned beyond the point of no return or committed a sin that is unforgivable. When that voice in your ear is telling you that it is a waste of your time to go to the Lord for forgiveness and that your Father has given up on you, just remember this. Our Father would have not sacrificed His only Son to be tortured and crucified, if you were not His most prized possession, who

He so passionately wants to come home to Him. Just as the father of the prodigal son, your Father is awaiting you with your robe, sandals and a feast to welcome you home.

The lifelong battle that we call recovery definitely does not have to be one of torture and temptation. If we drift away from the fellowship with others who share our passion in Christ and our walk in recovery, we will find ourselves struggling with the enemy's tricks and traps. However, if we remain in fellowship and get out of our selfish focuses, recovery is nothing less than a blissful walk with the Father. It is also at this time we can finally witness the amazing work of the Father as He takes what was meant for evil and to harm you and He uses it for good.

This is how we know love: Jesus laid down his life for us, and we ought to lay down our lives for our brothers and sisters. But if a person has material possessions and sees a brother or sister in need and that person doesn't care—how can the love of God remain in him?

Little children, let's not love with words or speech but with action and truth. This is how we will know that we belong to the truth and reassure our hearts in God's presence.

1John 3: 16-19 (CEB)

The good that will come from your fall to "rock bottom" and your struggles to climb out will be that of how you choose to allow God to use your experience to lift others up. Step Twelve will be the determining factor between a lifetime of sobriety or a relapse to death. It is when you will begin to develop an amazing awareness of self-confidence. Not one of arrogance and pride however, but one that is of assurance in God and that you are right where He called you to be and doing exactly what He has called you to do.

Most importantly, the final life-long step also involves the recovery of your relationships with your friends and family. It's no secret that addicts succeed in completely pulverizing any and all trust and confidence from those who love them. Just because we are walking among the clouds and feeling the natural highs from our newly-found freedom from our demons, it does not mean that those we hurt are feeling the same way. They have heard all of our lies and have fallen victim to our promises and tricks too many times. They are still hesitating in our past and just waiting for us to burst out of our sheep's clothing. Nothing we say or declare can change or sway their hesitation to believe us or give any credence to our words. It is a defensive wall we have forced them to build around their hardened hearts in order to avoid future heartbreaks and disappointments.

As we take our strides through Step 12, those we love and have hurt, will watch very carefully in anticipation of our next fall. At this point, it is so important that we have empathy and try to understand their doubt and insecurities. The very worst thing that can be done is to demonstrate anger or frustration in their disbelief and lack of trust. We earned that distrust over time, and it will take them time to start seeing and trusting the new you. Just as it takes all of us our own time to make it through the steps of recovery, our loved ones will begin opening back up on their own schedule and at their own pace. The only thing we can do is to remain in the focus of Steps 10 through 12 and allow our actions to do the talking. When we focus on reaching out to others and helping them pick up the pieces of their broken lives, we begin to give purpose to our lives once again. It is then we can turn a tragic time in our life into a meaningful experience we use the rest of our lives to bless others in our paths. In time, the trust will begin to rebuild, and a new form of love will begin to grow between you and your loved ones.

As for yourself, it is also at this step that you will finally find the ability to begin forgiving yourself and recognize how *"God works all things together for good for the ones who love God, for those who are called according to his purpose."*

Notes

Scripture quotations in this publication are from the Common English Bible © Copyright 2011 by the Common English Bible. All rights reserved. Used by permission. (www.CommonEnglishBible.com<http://www.CommonEnglishBible.com>)

Copyright © 1952, 1953, 1981 by Alcoholics Anonymous Publishing (now known as Alcoholics Anonymous World Services, Inc.) All rights reserved.

THE TWELVE STEPS OF ALCOHOLICS ANONYMOUS

1. We admitted we were powerless over alcohol—that our lives had become unmanageable.

2. Came to believe that a Power greater than ourselves could restore us to sanity.

3. Made a decision to turn our will and our lives over to the care of God as we understood Him.

4. Made a searching and fearless moral inventory of ourselves.

5. Admitted to God, to ourselves, and to another human being the exact nature of our wrongs.

6. Were entirely ready to have God remove all these defects of character.

7. Humbly asked Him to remove our shortcomings.

8. Made a list of all persons we had harmed, and became willing to make amends to them all.

9. Made direct amends to such people wherever possible, except when to do so would injure them or others.

10. Continued to take personal inventory and when we were wrong promptly admitted it.

11. Sought through prayer and meditation to improve our conscious contact with God, as we understood Him, praying only for knowledge of His will for us and the power to carry that out.

12. Having had a spiritual awakening as the result of these Steps, we tried to carry this message to alcoholics, and to practice these principles in all our affairs.

The Twelve Steps are reprinted with permission of Alcoholics Anonymous World Services, Inc. ("AAWS") Permission to reprint the Twelve Steps does not mean that AAWS has reviewed or approved the contents of this publication, or that AAWS necessarily agrees with the views expressed herein. A.A. is a program of recovery from alcoholism only - use of the Twelve Steps in connection with programs and activities which are patterned after A.A., but which address other problems, or in any other non-A.A. context, does not imply otherwise. Additionally, while A.A. is a spiritual program, A.A. is not a religious program. Thus, A.A. is not affiliated or allied with any sect, denomination, or specific religious belief. (Visit us on the web at aa.org)

LANIER T. NORTHRUP

CPSIA information can be obtained
at www.ICGtesting.com
Printed in the USA
LVHW021501030220
645678LV00014B/1345